SWEET LAYER CAKES™

Edited by Carolyn S. Vagts

Annie's®

Introduction

When precuts first came on the quilting scene, quilters weren't quite sure what to do with them other than buy and look at them. They're definitely eye candy. First, the 5" charm pack hit the shelves, and everyone loved them, but the odd measurement made it hard to incorporate them into existing patterns. Slowly, designers began to create patterns exclusively for them. Then the precut 2½"-strip roll took over.

This book is all about the use of 10" squares—aka Layer Cakes, Crackers, Treat Squares or Paddy Cakes—and I'm sure there are a few other names not mentioned here. Different manufacturers have different names, but no matter what these packs of 10" squares are called, they all work for projects in this book. Some of the patterns also use yardage, but all are designed around the use of 10" squares.

Now is the time to get out those 10" precut squares you've been stashing or make a trip to your local quilt shop and pick up a few. The designs in this book are mainly fast and easy, and many have size options. There's a pattern or two for everyone. We have all skill levels, some size options, designer tips and styles from contemporary to traditional.

Using 10" squares can be very fun and inspiring, so unleash your imagination, get out your Layer Cakes and get ready for a sweet treat!

All best,

Carolyn L. Vagts

Table of Contents

Sunburst Melody, ***page 15***

Cracked Ice, ***page 24***

Quick Chic

Designed by Gina Gempesaw
Machine-Quilted by Carole Whaling

Create a quick runner and matching place mats using precut 10" squares. These projects can be made in an afternoon.

Project Note

Materials given and cutting instructions will make one runner and two place mats.

Project Specifications

Skill Level: Beginner
Place Mat Size: 18½" x 14½"
Runner Size: 41" x 18½"

Materials

- 21 coordinating 10" squares
- ⅔ yard black solid
- 2⅓ yards backing
- Batting 49" x 26" and (2) 24" x 20"
- Thread
- Basic sewing tools and supplies

Cutting for Place Mat & Runner

1. Select nine 10" squares; subcut each square into four 5" A squares to total 36 A squares.

2. Select two light 10" squares for runner borders; subcut each square into two 3" x 9½" B rectangles and one 3" x 9¾" D rectangle.

3. Select two dark 10" squares for runner borders; subcut each square into two 3" x 9½" C rectangles and one 3" x 9¾" E rectangle.

4. Select four light 10" squares for place mat borders; subcut each square into one 3¼" x 9¾" I rectangle and one 3" F square.

5. Select four dark 10" squares for place mat borders; subcut each square into one each 3¼" x 9¾" H and 3" x 7" G rectangles.

6. Cut four 2¼" by fabric width black solid binding strips for runner.

7. Cut four 2¼" by fabric width black solid binding strips for place mats.

8. Cut one 26" x 49" rectangle along length of backing fabric for runner.

9. Cut two 20" x 24" rectangles backing fabric for place mats.

Completing the Runner

1. Select 24 A squares and the B, C, D and E rectangles.

2. Join eight A squares to make a horizontal row; press. Repeat to make three rows. Join the rows to complete the runner center; press.

3. Select and join two matching C and two matching B rectangles to make a top strip referring to Figure 1; press. Repeat to make the bottom strip.

Figure 1

4. Sew the top and bottom strips to the runner center referring to Figure 2; press.

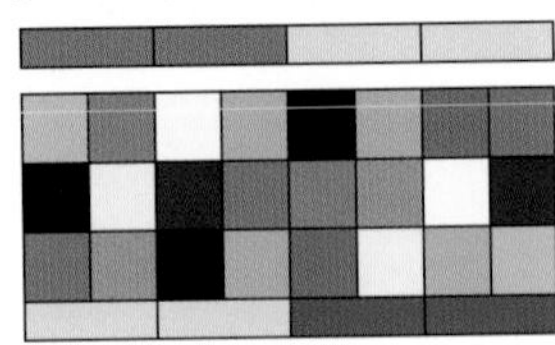
Figure 2

5. Select and join one each D and E rectangles to make an end strip; press. Repeat to make a second end strip.

6. Sew the end strips to opposite ends of the pieced center, matching B and D, and C and E fabrics at corners referring to Figure 3 to complete the runner top; press.

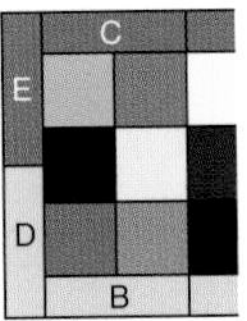

Figure 3

7. Layer, quilt and bind the runner referring to Finishing Your Quilt on page 48.

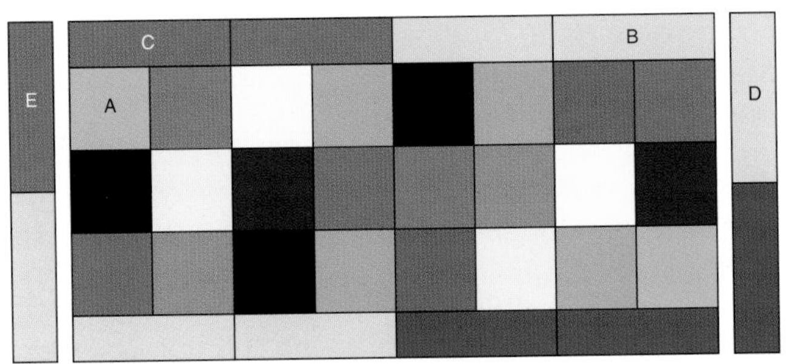

Quick Chic Runner
Assembly Diagram 41" x 18½"

Completing the Place Mats

1. To complete one place mat, select six assorted A squares, two different sets of one each matching G and H rectangles, and two different sets of one each matching F square and I rectangle.

2. Join three A squares to make a horizontal row; press. Repeat to make a second row. Join the rows to complete the place mat center; press.

3. Sew an F square to one G rectangle to make an end strip; press. Repeat to make a second end strip. Sew an end strip to opposite short ends of the pieced A center as shown in Figure 4; press.

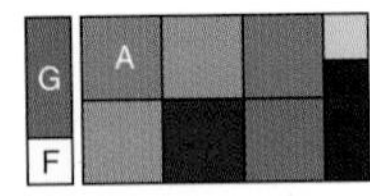

Figure 4

4. Referring to Figure 5, sew H to I on short ends to make a side strip; press. Repeat to make a second side strip. Sew a side strip to opposite sides of the pieced unit to complete the place mat top; press.

Figure 5

5. Layer, quilt and bind the place mat using two of the previously cut place mat binding strips referring to Finishing Your Quilt on page 48.

6. Repeat steps 1–5 to complete a second place mat. ■

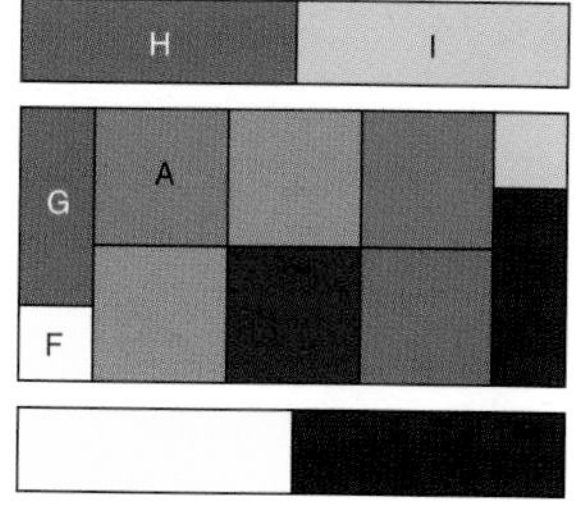

Quick Chic Place Mat
Assembly Diagram 18½" x 14½"

"I love the idea of using just the Layer Cake fabrics in a project." —Gina Gempesaw

Beanstalks

Design by Julie Weaver

Turn a collection of 10" squares into this fast and easy stylish quilt. The addition of solid sashing calms and defines the prints.

Project Specifications

- Skill Level: Beginner
- Quilt Size: 52" x 62"
- Block Size: 10" x 10"
- Number of Blocks: 20

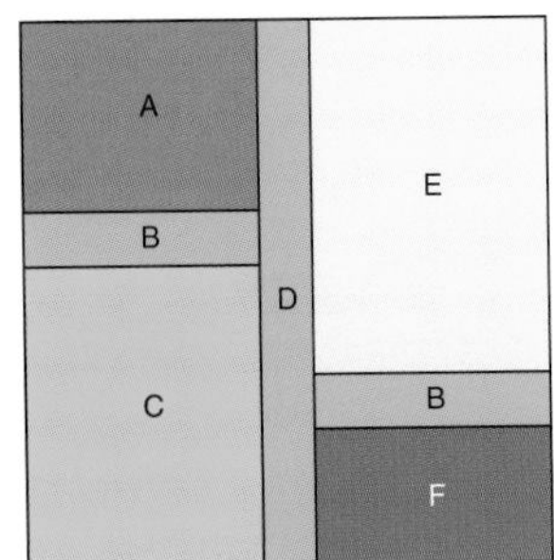

Beanstalk
10" x 10" Block
Make 20

Materials

- 20 coordinating precut 10" squares
- ½ yard green/aqua print
- 1⅛ yards green tonal
- 1¼ yards light green solid
- 4 yards backing
- Batting 60" x 70"
- Thread
- Basic sewing tools and supplies

Tip

The use of a solid fabric to separate the pieces and in the borders serves to calm the use of the various prints in the quilt itself. Using a solid color pulls all of the other fabrics together.

Cutting

1. Stack four or five precut 10" squares at a time and cut in half to make a total of 40 (5" x 10") rectangles; subcut as per instructions to make the A, C, E and F rectangles.

2. Cut five 2½" by fabric width K/L strips green/aqua print.

3. Cut 10 (1½" by fabric width) G/H/O/P strips green tonal.

4. Cut six 2¼" by fabric width binding strips green tonal.

5. Cut two 5" by fabric width strips light green solid; subcut into 40 (1½" x 5") B strips.

6. Cut one 10½" by fabric width strip light green solid; subcut into 20 (1½" x 10½") D rectangles.

7. Cut 10 (1½" by fabric width) I/J/M/N strips light green solid.

8. Cut two 70" by fabric width strips from backing fabric. Remove selvage edges, join along the 70" lengths and trim to 60" x 70" to make a backing with vertical seams.

Completing the Blocks

1. From one 5" x 10" rectangle, cut one each 5" x 4" A and 5" x 6" C rectangle as shown in Figure 1.

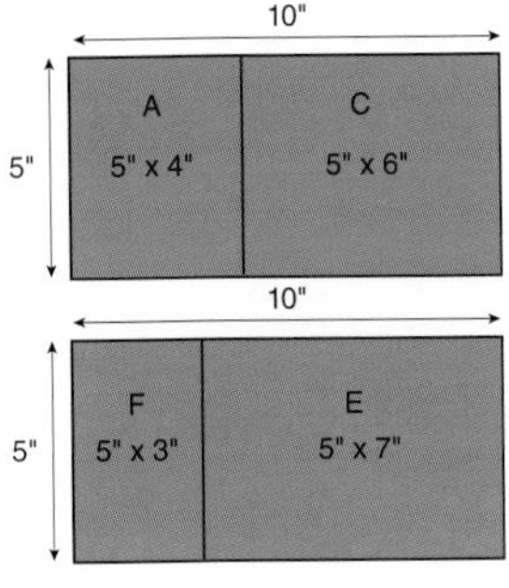

Figure 1

2. From the second 5" x 10" rectangle of the same fabric, cut one each 5" x 7" E and 5" x 3" F rectangle, again referring to Figure 1.

3. Repeat steps 1 and 2 with all 5" x 10" rectangles.

Tip

This quilt can be adapted easily to any color scheme or theme. It's a good pattern for using up lots of precut 10" squares. Pay careful attention when cutting the squares. In order to achieve the design, each square must be cut accurately. Stacking the pieces side by side as each square was cut and then mixing the order up after cutting made selecting assorted fabrics for each block easier. Mixing fabrics is sometimes the hardest part.

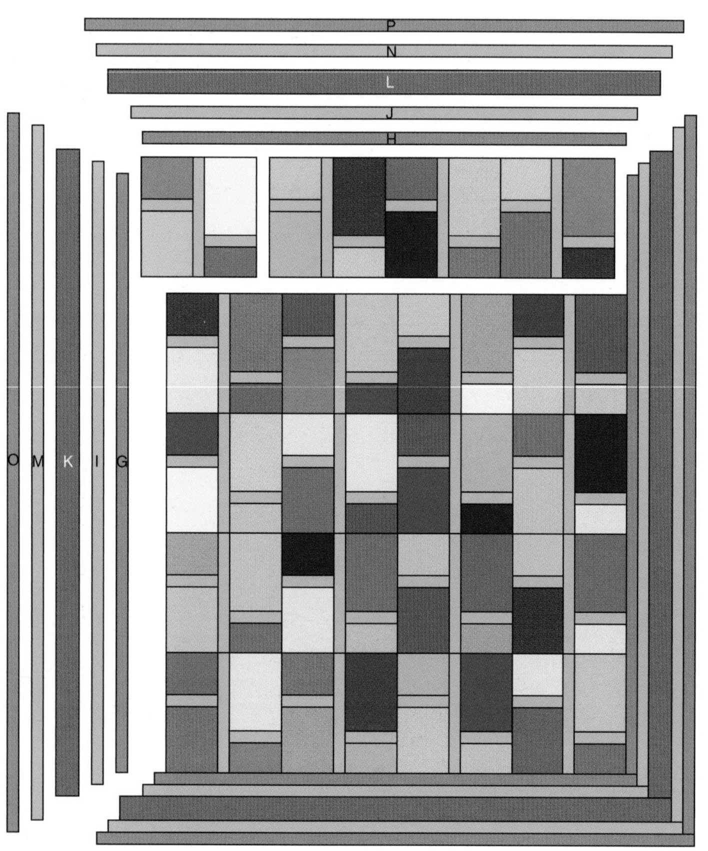

Beanstalks
Assembly Diagram 52" x 62"

4. To complete one Beanstalk block, select one each A, C, E and F rectangle of different fabrics, one D rectangle and two B strips.

5. Join A and C with B, and E and F with B as shown in Figure 2; press seams toward B.

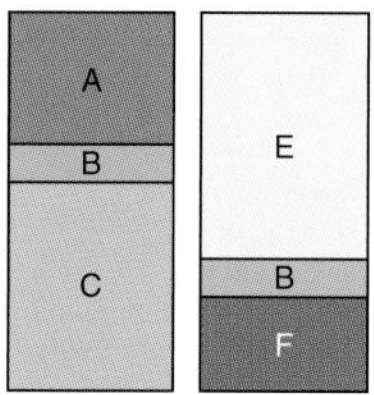

Figure 2

6. Join the A-B-C unit and the E-B-F unit with D to complete one Beanstalk block referring to Figure 3; press seams toward D.

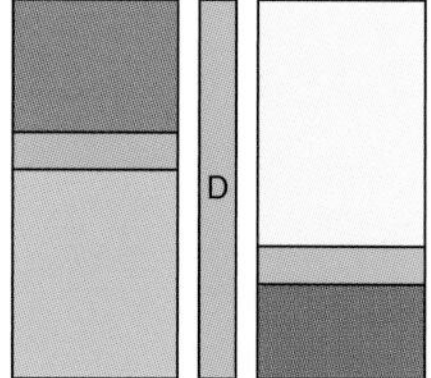

Figure 3

7. Repeat steps 4–6 to complete a total of 20 Beanstalk blocks.

Completing the Quilt

1. Select and join four Beanstalk blocks to make a row referring to the Assembly Diagram; press. Repeat to make a total of five rows.

2. Join the rows to complete the pieced center; press.

3. Join the G/H/M/N strips to make a long strip; press. Subcut strip into two each 1½" x 50½" G, 1½" x 42½" H, 1½" x 60½" O and 1½" x 52½" P strips.

4. Join the K/L strips to make a long strip; press. Subcut strip into two 2½" x 54½" K strips and two 2½" x 48½" L strips.

5. Join the I/J/M/N strips to make a long strip; press. Subcut strip into two each 1½" x 52½" I, 1½" x 44½" J, 1½" x 58½" M and 1½" x 50½" N strips.

6. Complete the quilt top referring to the Assembly Diagram adding the strips cut in steps 3–5 to opposite sides and then the top and bottom of the pieced center in alphabetical order, pressing seams toward newly added strips as you sew.

7. Layer, quilt and bind referring to Finishing Your Quilt on page 48. ■

"I like making smaller-size quilts that are easy and quick. I am always thinking of quilts I can give as gifts—especially when a new baby (or two or three) is expected. Since we all have fabric we need to use, and so we can justify buying more, this one could also be a scrap quilt with the solid 'stalks' pulling the whole thing together." —Julie Weaver

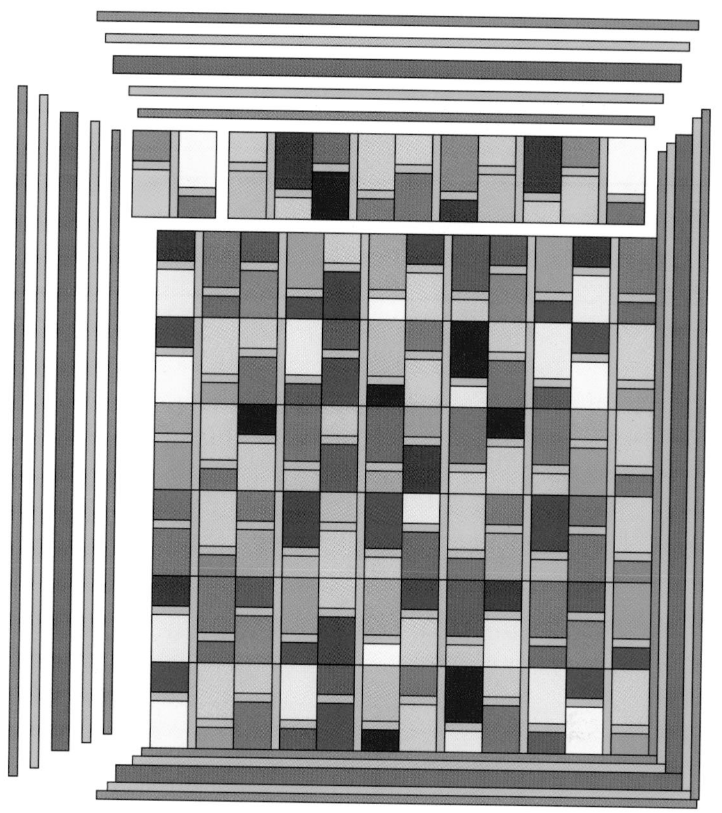

Beanstalks Alternate Size
Assembly Diagram 72" x 82"
Make 22 more blocks and join in 7 rows of 6 blocks each to create a bed-size quilt using the same-width border strips as the smaller-size quilt. Remember to increase fabric yardages to make this larger-size quilt.

Tip

A great way to mix fabrics randomly is to place each stack of same-size pieces in a separate paper bag. Then reach your hand inside and take one piece from each bag. Put back one piece if you select the same fabric twice, but otherwise, make a rule to use your picks no matter what. This takes all of the decisions regarding trying to coordinate fabrics out of the equation.

Pop of Color Bed Runner & Pillow

Design by Chris Malone

A collection of 10" squares and some buttons are sometimes all you need to create a stunning bed runner and pillow.

Project Specifications

- Skill Level: Confident Beginner
- Runner Size: 84" x 24"
- Pillow Size: 15¾" x 15¾"
- Block Size: 8½" x 8½"
- Number of Blocks: 7 for runner

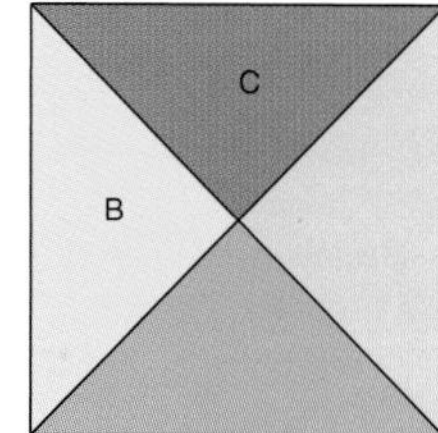

Hourglass
8½" x 8½" Block
Make 7

Bed Runner

Materials

- 38 coordinating 10" precut squares
- ⅜ yard burgundy/tan dot
- 2¾ yards backing
- Batting 92" x 32"
- Thread to match fabrics
- Hand-quilting thread to match yo-yo fabrics
- 12 (⅞"-diameter) cover buttons
- Compass or 10"-diameter object
- Basic sewing tools and supplies

Cutting

1. Cut six 2¼" by fabric width binding strips burgundy/tan dot.

2. Cut one 32" x 92" strip along length of the backing fabric.

Completing the Hourglass Blocks

1. Separate the 10" precut squares into 14 dark (A) yo-yo backgrounds, six light (B), six medium (C) and 12 light (D) for yo-yos. Set aside two dark A squares to use for covering buttons.

2. Draw a diagonal line from corner to corner on the wrong side of each B square.

3. Pin a B square and a C square right sides together and stitch ¼" from each side of the drawn line referring to Figure 1.

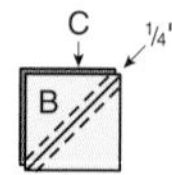

Figure 1

4. Cut apart on the drawn line and open each half to make two B-C units as shown in Figure 2; press seam toward C.

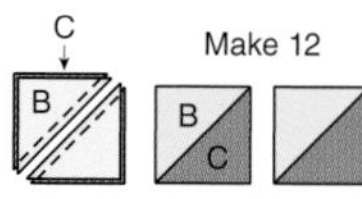

Figure 2

5. Repeat steps 3 and 4 with remaining B and C triangles to make a total of 12 B-C units.

6. Cut each B-C unit in half from corner to corner to make a total of 24 B-C units, cutting across the seam as shown in Figure 3.

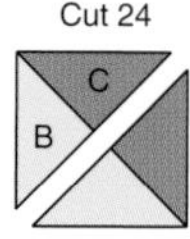

Figure 3

7. Mix up the B-C units and arrange seven pairs so the light and dark of different fabrics alternate referring to Figure 4. Set aside the remaining 10 B-C units to use for outer setting triangles.

Figure 4

8. Sew the paired B-C units together on the cut diagonal edge to make seven Hourglass blocks referring to Figure 5. Check the size of the completed blocks. Carefully trim to an even 9" square, keeping the diagonal seams centered, again referring to Figure 5. ***Note:*** *If your completed Hourglass blocks are smaller than 9" x 9", just trim to the next size down. The runner will be slightly smaller than the sample shown.*

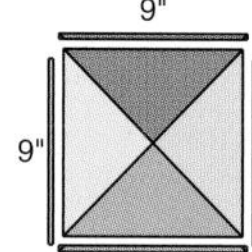

Figure 5

9. Trim the dark A squares to 9" square to match the size of the Hourglass blocks. ***Note:*** *Cut the A squares to the same size as the Hourglass blocks referring to note in step 8.*

Tip

There are several ways to attach yo-yos to a quilt. The yo-yos in this project are sewn on by hand with a running stitch that goes through all layers, making it a quilting stitch as well. It slightly flattens the edges. If you use an invisible hand-appliqué stitch, you will have a puffier yo-yo. Alternately, you can sew them down by machine using a straight stitch close to the edge or use a blanket stitch, which will flatten them a little more. It is a matter of preference about how you want the yo-yos to look when they are finished.

Completing the Bed Runner

1. Referring to Figure 6, arrange and join the A squares, Hourglass blocks and B-C units in seven diagonal rows.

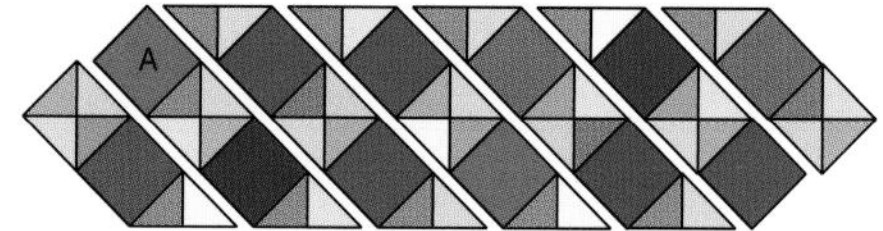

Figure 6

2. Join the rows referring to the Placement Diagram to complete the runner top.

3. Trim the runner edges to ¼" beyond the intersections of the seams as shown in Figure 7.

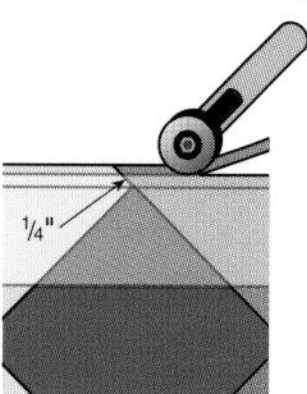

Figure 7

4. Because runner outer edges are bias and will stretch, carefully machine-stitch ⅛" from all edges.

5. Layer, quilt and bind referring to Finishing Your Quilt on page 48.

6. Follow the manufacturer's instructions to cover the buttons with fabric circles from the remaining 10" dark A squares.

7. Cut a 10"-diameter circle from each of the 12 D squares. ***Note:*** *Use a compass to draw a circle pattern, or find a bowl or plate that is approximately 10" across.*

8. Finger-press ⅛"–¼" hem along the outer edge of one fabric circle and use a double strand of matching thread to hand-sew gathering stitches close to the folded edge all around, making stitches about ¼" long and ¼" apart as shown in Figure 8.

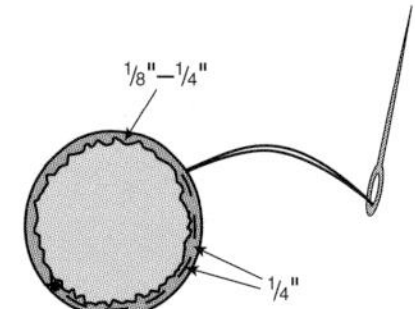

Figure 8

Pop of Color Bed Runner
Placement Diagram 84" x 24"

9. Pull the thread to gather the edges together, forming a small hole. Push the hole to the center, and knot and clip the thread to complete one yo-yo as shown in Figure 9.

Figure 9

10. Using a double strand of matching thread, sew a covered button to the center of a yo-yo; sew the button and yo-yo to the center of an A square as shown in Figure 10.

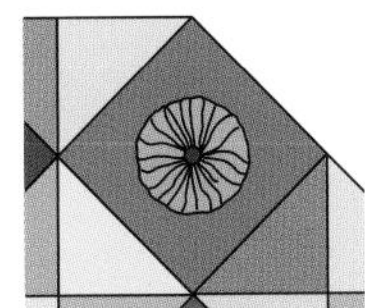

Figure 10

11. Use one strand of quilting thread to sew the edges of the yo-yo to the A square with a running stitch through all layers referring to Figure 11.

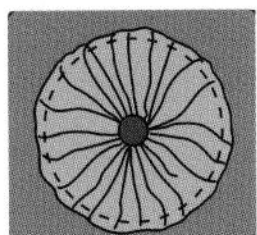

Figure 11

12. Repeat steps 8–11 with remaining circles to complete the bed runner.

Pillow

Materials

- 19 coordinating 10" precut squares
- ½ yard backing
- 20"-square batting
- All-purpose thread
- Hand-quilting thread to match yo-yo fabrics
- 9 (¾"-diameter) cover buttons
- Compass or 6"-diameter object
- 16"-square pillow form
- Basic sewing tools and supplies

Cutting

1. Cut nine 5¾" B squares from nine medium/dark 10" precut squares.

2. Cut 9 (6"-diameter) circles from nine light 10" precut squares.

3. Cut two 23½" x 16¼" backing rectangles.

Completing the Pillow

1. Arrange and join the B squares into three rows of three B squares each; press seams open. Join the rows to complete the pillow top.

2. Baste the pieced pillow top right side up on top of the batting square; quilt as desired.

3. Follow the manufacturer's instructions to cover the buttons with circles from leftover fabrics.

4. Complete nine yo-yos from the light circles, add covered buttons and sew a yo-yo circle to the center of each B square referring to steps 8–11 of Completing the Bed Runner.

5. Press and sew a double ¼" hem on one long edge of each backing rectangle.

6. Pin and baste the hemmed backing rectangles to the quilted pillow top with right sides together, matching raw edges and overlapping in the center as shown in Figure 12.

Figure 12

7. Stitch all around edges using a ¼" seam allowance. Clip corners and turn right side out through the opening created by the overlapped backing rectangles.

8. Insert pillow form to finish. ■

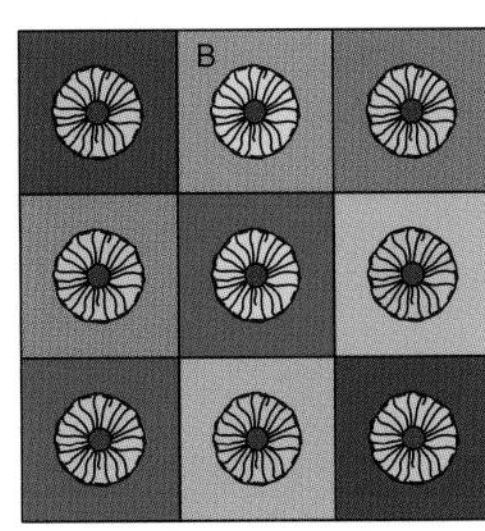

Pop of Color Pillow
Placement Diagram 15¾" x 15¾"

"When you make a bed runner or pillow, as opposed to a bed quilt, you can add some fun features that might be impractical on the larger piece. Yo-yos with fabric-covered buttons are an impressive embellishment that really change the look of the patchwork." —Chris Malone

Sunburst Melody

Design by Wendy Sheppard

Let this paper-pieced beauty be your next project. A couple of coordinating prints and a collection of 10" squares of solids or tonals will be sufficient to complete the blocks.

Project Specifications

- Skill Level: Intermediate
- Quilt Size: 52" x 52"
- Block Size: 7" x 7"
- Number of Blocks: 25

Materials

- 3 (total 48) precut 10" squares each of the following solid colors: royal blue, sky blue, olive, dark olive, green, lime green, purple, lavender, orange, yellow, red, coral, pink and light pink
- 4 (total 8) precut 10" squares each black and gray solids
- ⅜ yard white-with-multicolored polka dot
- ⅝ yard pink solid
- ⅝ yard white-with-floral print
- 1 yard cream solid
- 1½ yards cream-with-multicolored print
- 3½ yards backing
- Batting 60" x 60"
- Thread
- Template material
- Paper
- Basic sewing tools and supplies

Cutting

1. Cut B pieces for paper piecing from 10" precut squares as per pattern and instructions.

2. Cut A pieces from 10" precut squares as per pattern and instructions.

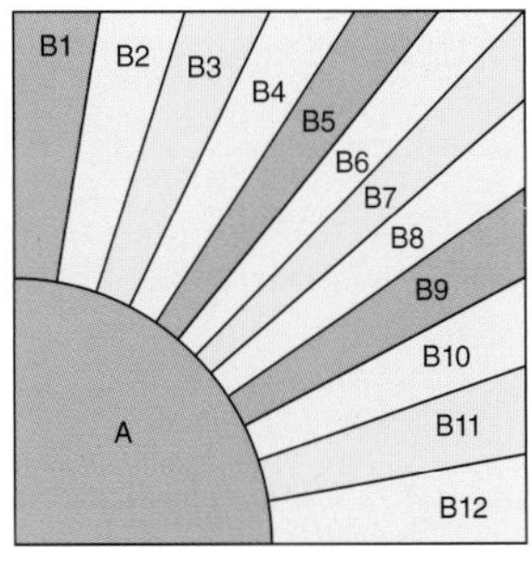

Orange/Yellow Sunburst
7" x 7" Block
Make 3

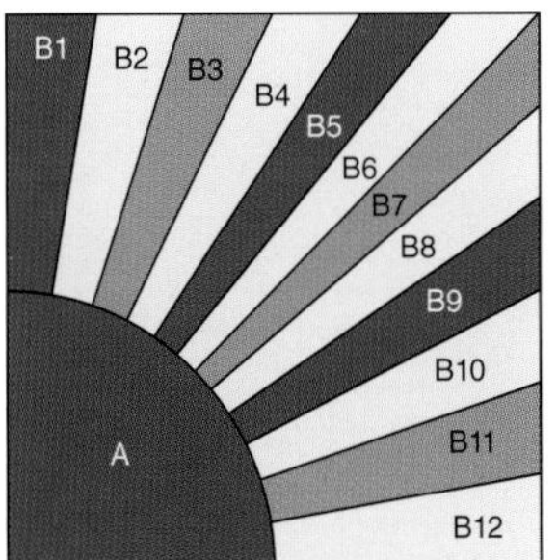

Black/Gray Sunburst
7" x 7" Block
Make 4

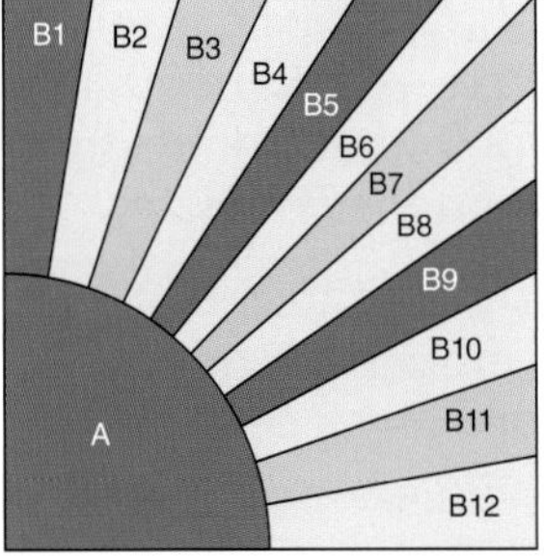

Royal Blue/Sky Blue Sunburst
7" x 7" Block
Make 3

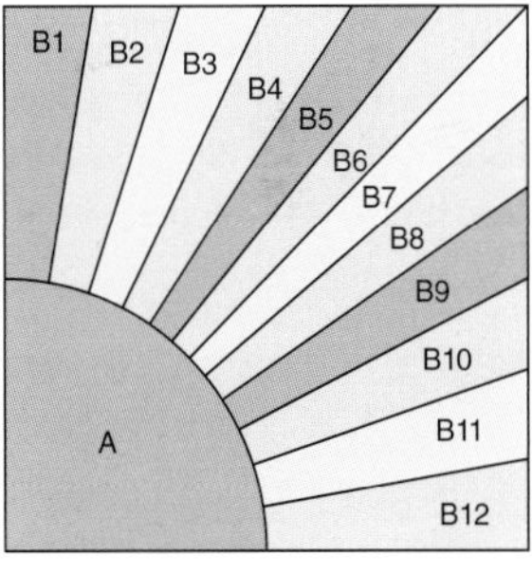

Pink/Light Pink Sunburst
7" x 7" Block
Make 3

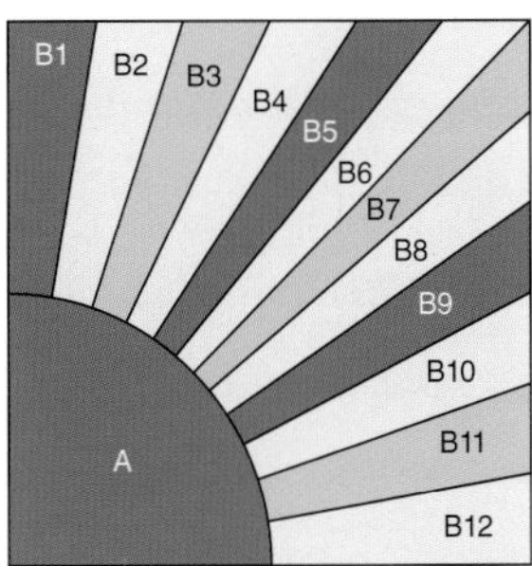

Green/Lime Green Sunburst
7" x 7" Block
Make 3

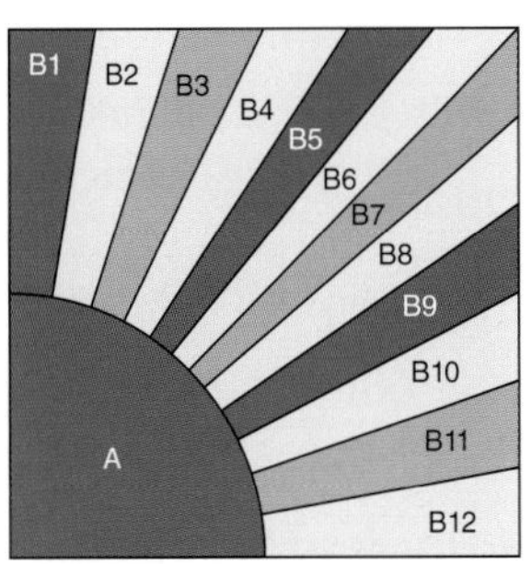

Purple/Lavender Sunburst
7" x 7" Block
Make 3

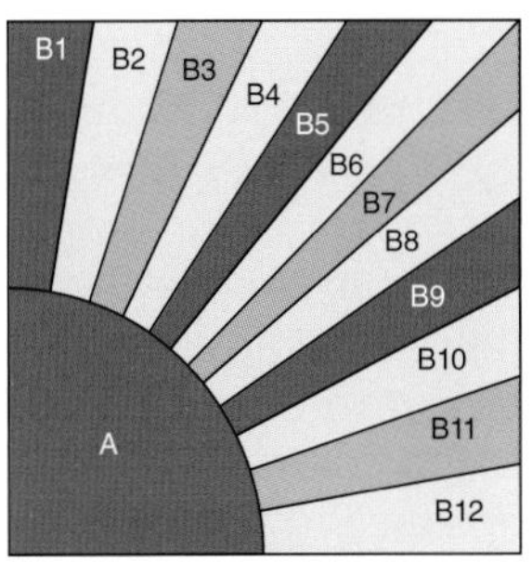

Red/Coral Sunburst
7" x 7" Block
Make 3

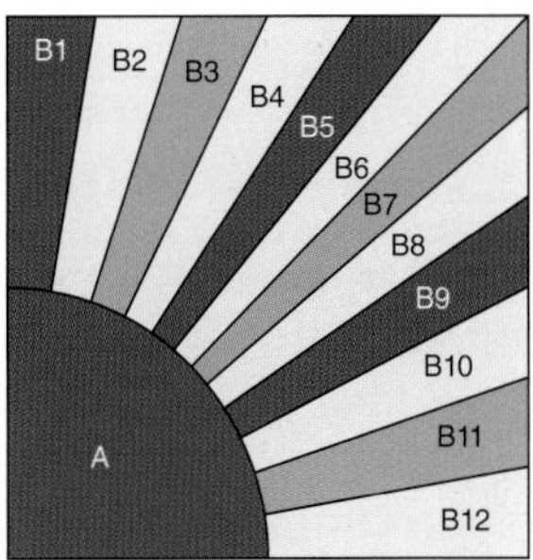

Dark Olive/Olive Sunburst
7" x 7" Block
Make 3

3. Cut two 2" x 41½" F strips white-with-multicolored polka dot.

4. Cut three 2" by fabric width G strips white-with-multicolored polka dot.

5. Cut six 2¼" by fabric width binding strips pink solid.

6. Cut five 3½" by fabric width J/K strips white-with-floral print.

7. Cut one 7½" by fabric width strip cream solid; subcut into 20 (1½" x 7½") C strips.

8. Cut six 1½" x 39½" D strips cream solid.

9. Cut two 1½" x 41½" E strips cream solid.

10. Cut five 1½" by fabric width H/I strips cream solid.

11. Cut background pieces for paper piecing from cream-with-multicolored print as per pattern and instructions.

12. Cut two 60" by fabric width strips backing fabric. Remove selvage, join strips along the 60" lengths and trim to 60" x 60" to make a backing with vertical or horizontal seams.

Completing the Blocks

1. Prepare templates for A and each B piece in the paper-piecing pattern using the full-size patterns given. When tracing the B pieces, remember that no seam allowance has been added to the long edges. Mark the piece letter/number on the templates.

2. Generously cut the B fabric pieces to add at least a ¼" seam allowance all around as shown in Figure 1. It is not necessary for allowance to be perfectly even all around as long as it is at least ¼".

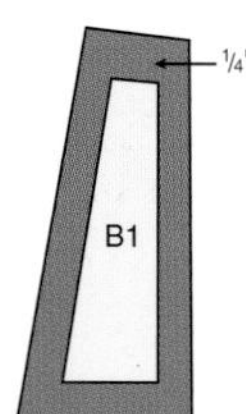

Figure 1

3. Cut three each B3, B7 and B11 from each of the following colors: sky blue, light pink, yellow, coral, olive, lime green and lavender. Cut three each B1, B5 and B9 from each of the following colors: royal blue, pink, orange, red, dark olive, green and purple.

4. Cut four each B3, B7 and B11 gray.

5. Cut four each B1, B5 and B9 black.

6. Cut 25 background pieces each B2, B4, B6, B8, B10 and B12 from cream-with-multicolored print.

7. Make 25 copies of the paper-piecing pattern and transfer all information.

8. To complete one black/gray block, select one black A, one each black B1, B5 and B9, one each gray B3, B7 and B11, and one each B2, B4, B6, B8, B10 and B12 background pieces.

9. Starting with the black B1 piece, place the piece wrong side together with the unmarked side of the paper-piecing pattern under the B1 area marked on the front of the pattern making sure that the B1 piece covers the entire area, including at least a ¼" seam allowance as shown in Figure 2; pin to hold.

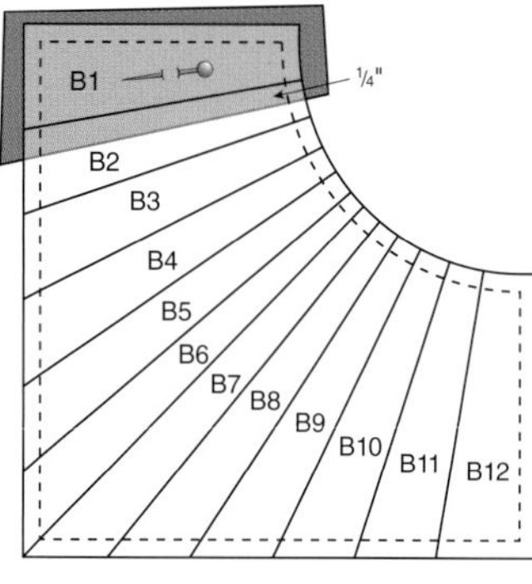

Figure 2

Tip

Use a 90/14 needle and reduce stitch size to 15–18 stitches per inch to help make paper removal easier later. Cut pieces at least ¼" larger than the space you will be covering—bigger is better. After stitching, trim all the excess to a ⅛–¼" seam allowance. Do not use steam when pressing the stitched units as it causes the paper to curl. If using a copier to make your copies, be sure to compare the original pattern to the copy for size. In addition, the copier ink may bleed into fabrics or onto your ironing surface, so protect the surface before ironing your paper-pieced sections.

10. Pin the B2 background piece right sides together with the B1 piece along the long inside seam; flip over to make sure it will cover the B2 area with extra for seams. Flip B2 back over B1 and turn the paper over; stitch on the line between pieces B1 and B2 as shown in Figure 3.

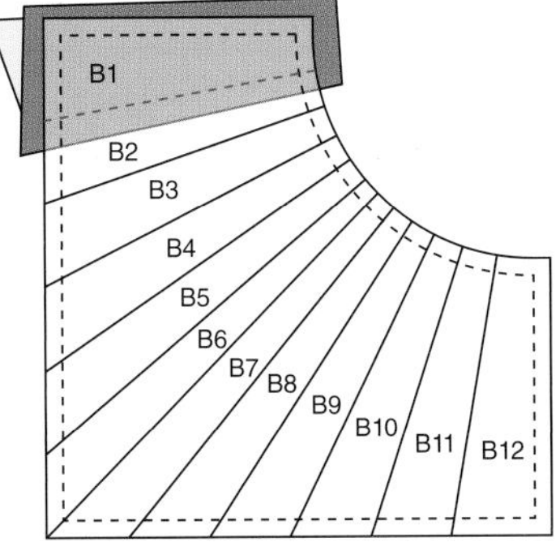

Figure 3

11. Flip piece B2 to the right side and finger-press flat along seam; pin to the paper referring to Figure 4.

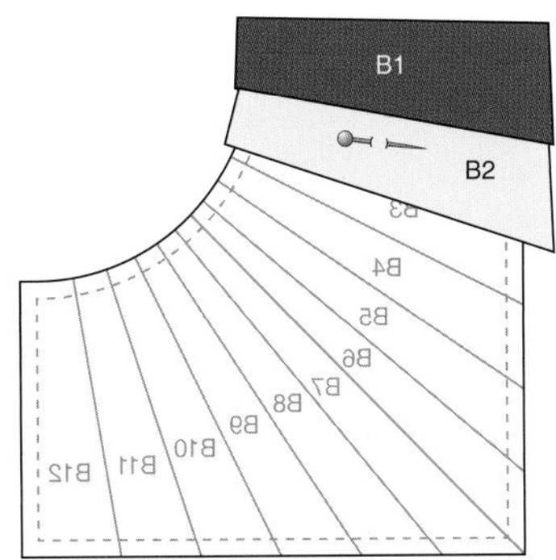

Figure 4

12. Repeat steps 9–11, continuing to add the B pieces to the paper foundation in numerical order to completely cover the paper foundation as shown in Figure 5.

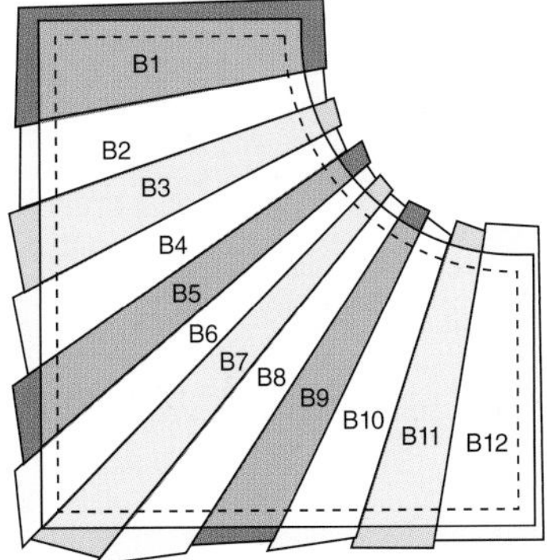

Figure 5

13. Trim the stitched section along the solid outer line edge of the paper-piecing pattern to complete one black/gray section as shown in Figure 6.

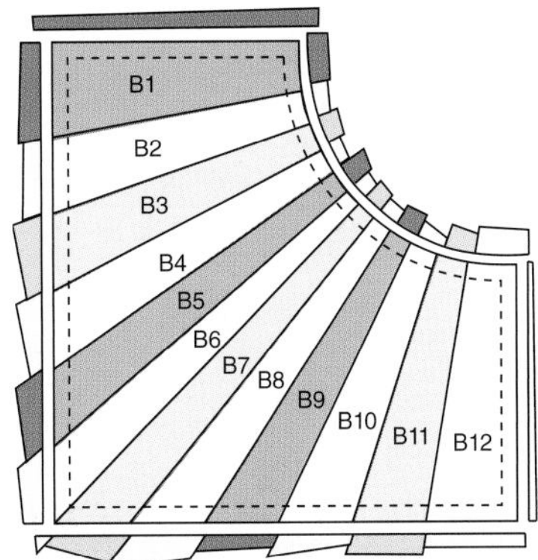

Figure 6

14. Sew the black A piece to the pieced section to complete one Black/Gray Sunburst block, matching notch on A to center seam between B6 and B7 of the paper-pieced section as shown in Figure 7; press seam toward A.

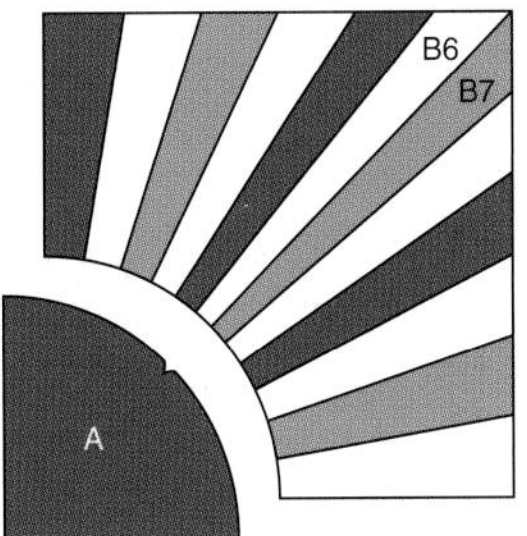

Figure 7

15. Repeat steps 8–14 to complete a total of four Black/Gray blocks and three each Royal Blue/Sky Blue, Dark Olive/Olive, Green/Lime Green, Red/Coral, Pink/Light Pink, Orange/Yellow and Purple/Lavender Sunburst blocks referring to the block drawings for color placement in blocks.

Completing the Quilt

1. Arrange and join five Sunburst blocks with four C strips to make a block row referring to the Assembly Diagram for block orientation in the row; press seams toward C strips.

2. Repeat step 1 to make a total of five rows, again referring to the Assembly Diagram for orientation of blocks in each row.

3. Join the block rows with four D strips to complete the pieced center; press seams toward D strips.

4. Remove paper from all blocks.

5. Sew D strips to the top and bottom, and E strips opposite sides of the pieced center; press seams toward D and E strips.

6. Sew F strips to the top and bottom of the pieced center; press seams toward F. Join the G strips on short ends to make a long strip; press. Subcut strip into two 2" x 44½" G strips. Sew these strips to opposite sides of the pieced center.

7. Join the H/I strips on short ends to make a long strip; press. Subcut strip into two 1½" x 44½" H strips and two 1½" x 46½" I strips.

8. Sew H strips to the top and bottom, and I strips to opposite sides of the pieced center; press seams toward H and I strips.

9. Join the J/K strips on short ends to make a long strip; press. Subcut strip into two 3½" x 46½" J strips and two 3½" x 52½" K strips.

10. Sew J strips to the top and bottom, and K strips to opposite sides of the pieced center to complete the quilt top; press seams toward J and K strips.

11. Layer, quilt and bind referring to Finishing Your Quilt on page 48. ■

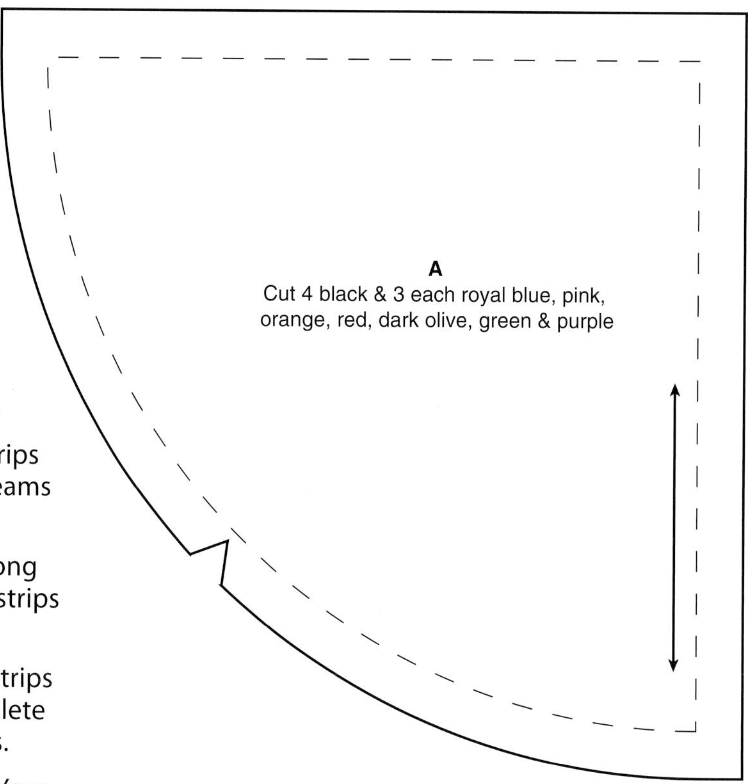

Sunburst Melody
Assembly Diagram 52" x 52"

Sunburst Melody Alternate Size
Assembly Diagram 64" x 88"
Make 29 more blocks and cut 25 more sashing strips. Join in 9 rows of 6 blocks each to create a bed-size quilt using 5"-wide outer border strips for the larger-size quilt. Remember to increase fabric yardages to make this larger-size quilt.

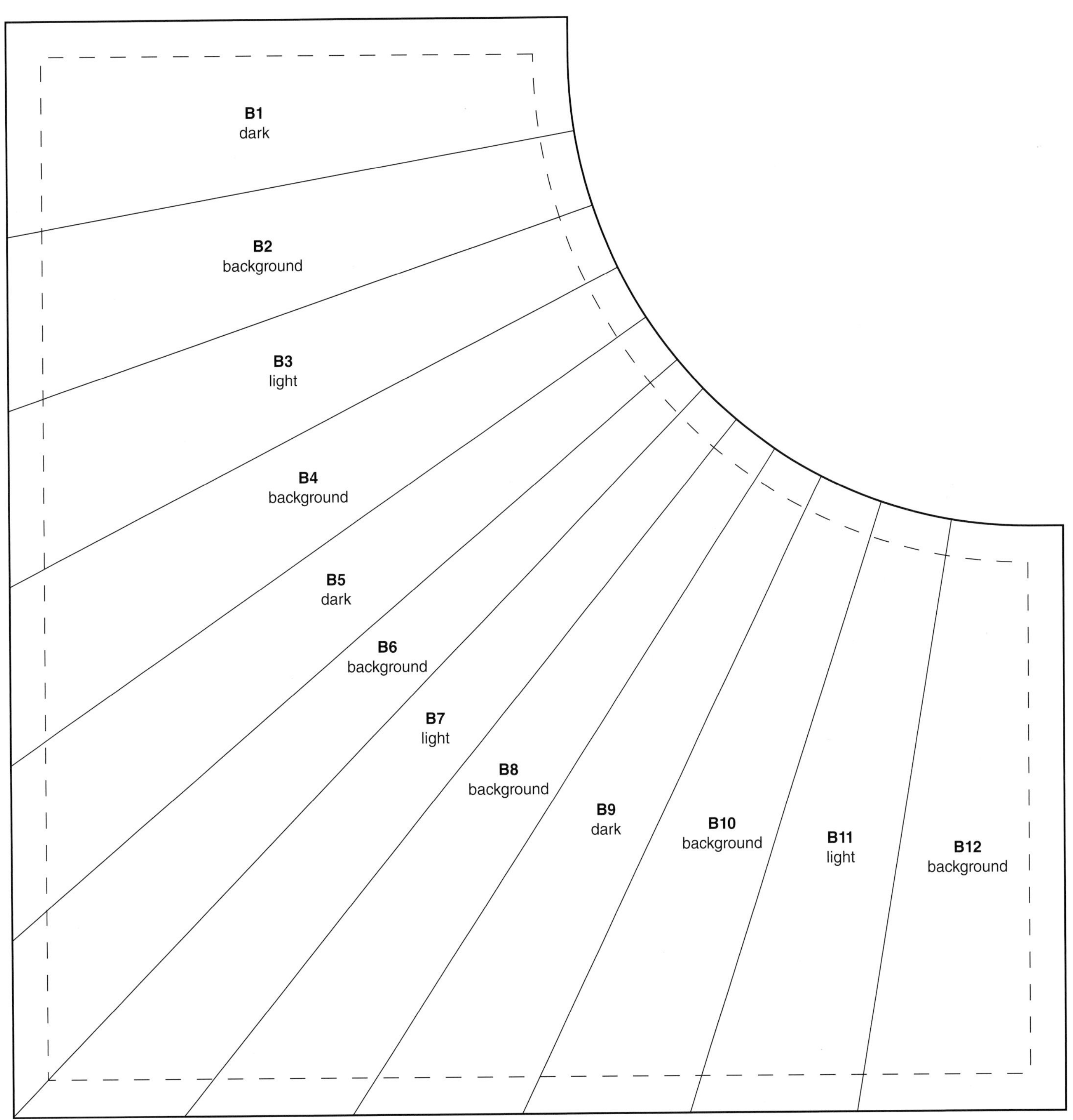

Sunburst Paper-Piecing Pattern
Make 25 copies

Sparkling Spools

Design by Missy Shepler

Colorful spools emerge at the block intersections when stitched together. This is a quick and easy project that only looks complicated.

Project Specifications

- Skill Level: Confident Beginner
- Quilt Size: 57" x 76"
- Block Size: 9½" x 9½"
- Number of Blocks: 48

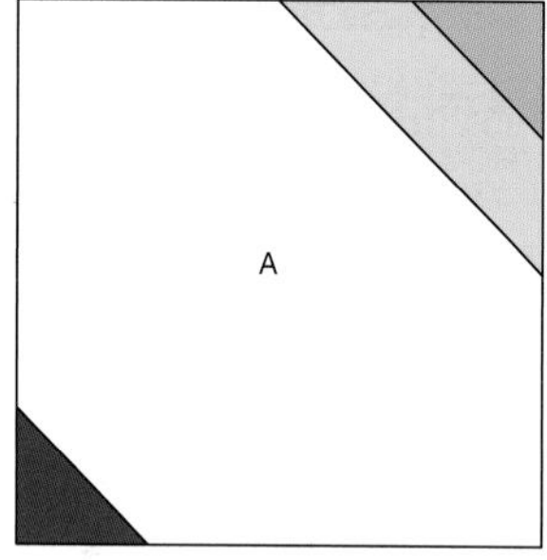

Sparkling Spools
9½" x 9½" Block
Make 48

Materials

- 22 assorted precut 10" batik squares
- ⅝ yard red batik
- 3⅔ yards white solid
- 4⅞ yards backing
- Batting 65" x 84"
- Thread
- Template material
- Clear acrylic 10" square ruler
- Clear acrylic rotary ruler and rotary cutter
- Clear tape
- Basic sewing tools and supplies

Cutting

1. Cut seven 2¼" by fabric width binding strips red batik.

2. Cut 12 (10" by fabric width) strips white solid; subcut into 48 (10") A squares.

3. Cut two 84" by fabric width strips backing fabric. Remove selvage edges, join along the 84" lengths and trim to 65" x 84" to make a backing with vertical seams.

Completing the Blocks

1. Trace the corner pattern given onto template material; transfer all pattern markings to the template. Carefully cut out the template on the solid outer line.

2. Tape the template right side up anywhere on the underside of the clear acrylic rotary ruler, aligning the long outer A edge with the ruler's edge as shown in Figure 1. The template should be right side up when you look at the right side of the ruler.

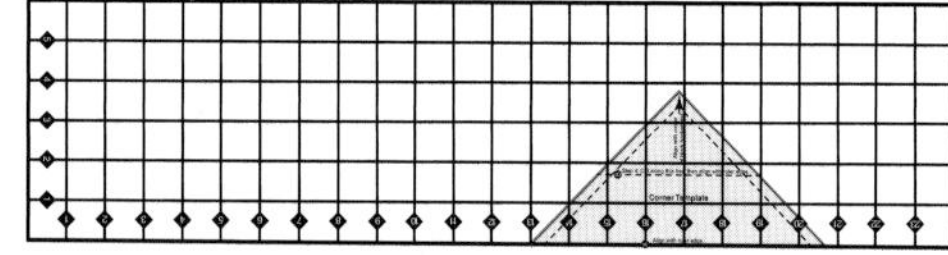

Figure 1

3. Place the template on the wrong side of one A square, aligning the template corner with one corner of the square. Using the template as a guide, mark seam line A as shown in Figure 2; repeat on all A squares.

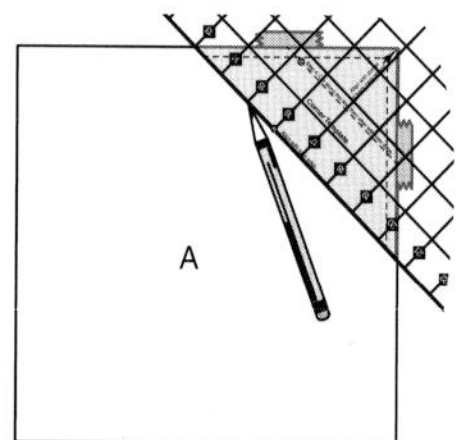

Figure 2

4. Place one precut batik square right sides together with one marked A square, aligning the outer edges. Stitch along the marked line as shown in Figure 3.

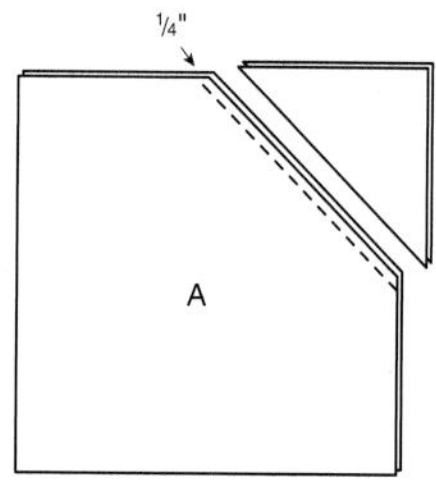

Figure 3

5. Use a rotary cutter and ruler to trim the seam allowance to ¼", making sure to cut on the side of the seam closest to the corner, again referring to Figure 3 on page 20; press seam open.

6. Remove the template from the ruler and cut the template into two pieces along seam line B. Set aside the triangle section to use later. Tape the rectangle section of the template to the underside of the ruler, aligning the edge marked seam line B with the ruler's edge.

7. Place the ruler on the wrong side of the block, aligning the long A edge of the template with the seam sewn in step 4; mark seam line B as shown in Figure 4.

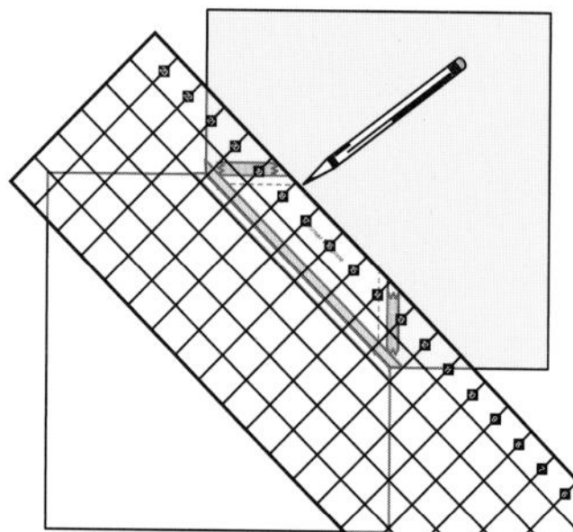

Figure 4

8. Place a different precut batik square right sides together with the marked block, making sure that the precut square aligns with or extends slightly beyond the A square's edges as shown in Figure 5.

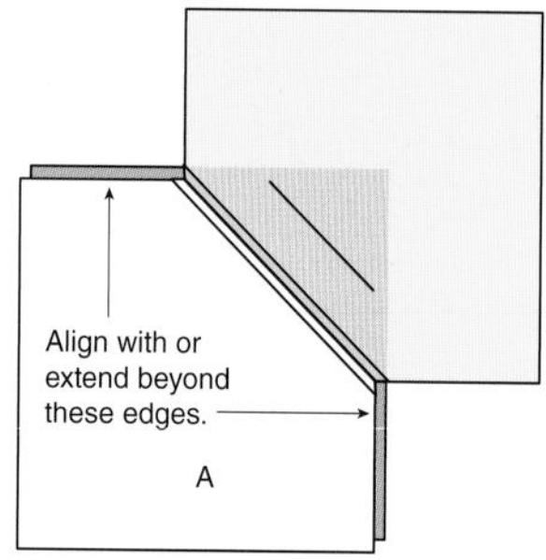

Figure 5

9. Stitch along the marked line. Use a rotary cutter and ruler to trim the seam allowance to ¼", making sure to cut on the side of the seam closest to the corner as shown in Figure 6; press the seam open.

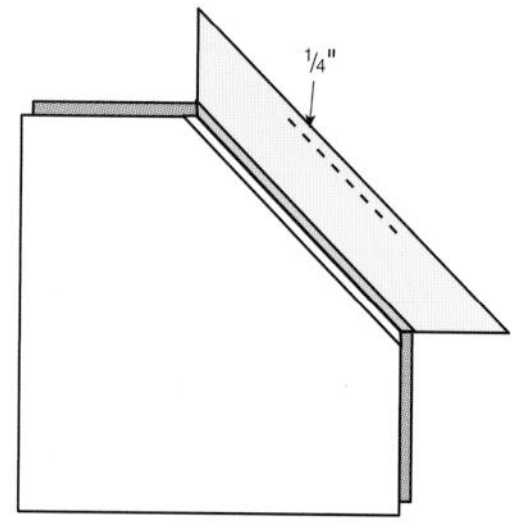

Figure 6

10. Align the 10"-square ruler with the edges of the A square; trim excess fabric from the block as shown in Figure 7. ***Note:*** *Be careful to keep the trimmed pieces as large as possible for use in subsequent blocks.*

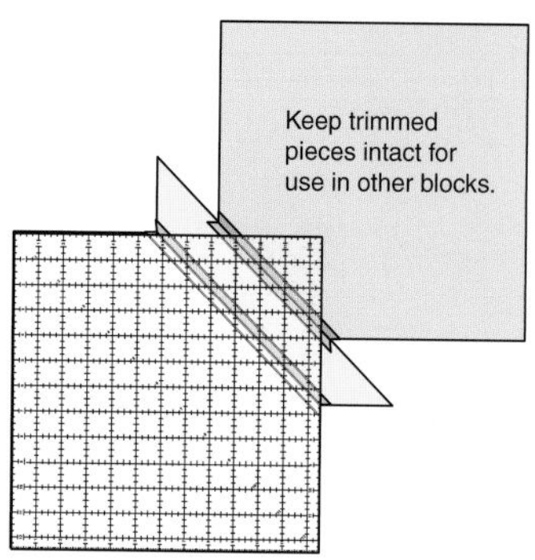

Figure 7

11. Repeat steps 4–10 to make a total of 48 blocks with one finished corner.

Tip

Make batches of 10–15 blocks, so there are plenty of trimmed pieces to choose from when making subsequent blocks.

12. Remove the template from the ruler. Tape the triangle section of the template to the underside of the ruler, aligning the edge marked seam line B with the ruler's edge.

13. Place the ruler on the wrong side of one trimmed block, aligning the corner of the template with the corner opposite the previously stitched pieces; mark the B seam line. Repeat this process on all 48 blocks.

14. Place a precut batik square, or trimmed scrap from a batik square that was already used, right sides together with one marked block, making sure to overlap the marked line and block edges by at least ¼". Stitch along the marked line. Use a rotary cutter and ruler to trim the seam to ¼", making sure to cut on the side of the seam closest to the corner; press seam open as shown in Figure 8.

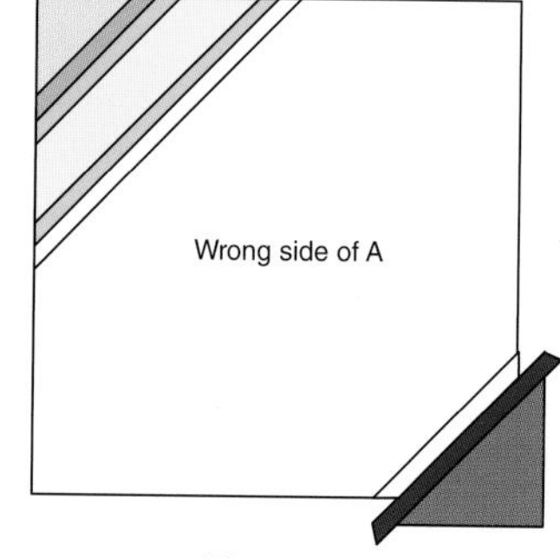

Figure 8

15. Using the 10" square ruler, trim the excess fabric from the block to make a 10" square to complete the block as shown in Figure 9.

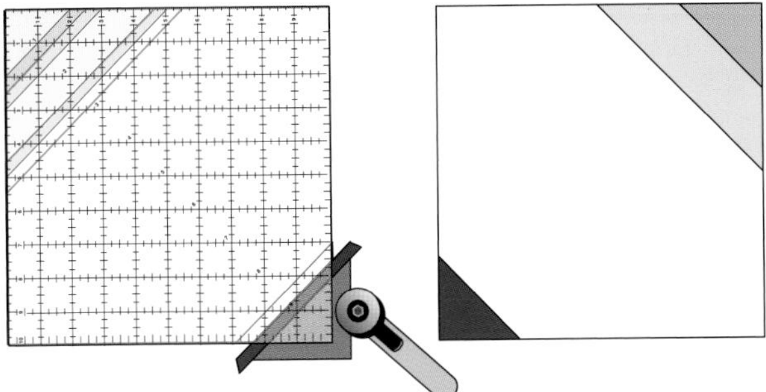

Figure 9

Tip

Taping the template to your rotary ruler makes measurement worries disappear! Just mark, sew and trim!

Sparkling Spools
Assembly Diagram 57" x 76"

16. Repeat steps 14 and 15 to complete a total of 48 Spool blocks.

Completing the Quilt

1. Arrange and join six blocks to make a row referring to the Assembly Diagram; press. Repeat to make eight rows.

2. Join the rows referring to the Assembly Diagram to complete the quilt top.

3. Layer, quilt and bind referring to Finishing Your Quilt on page 48. ■

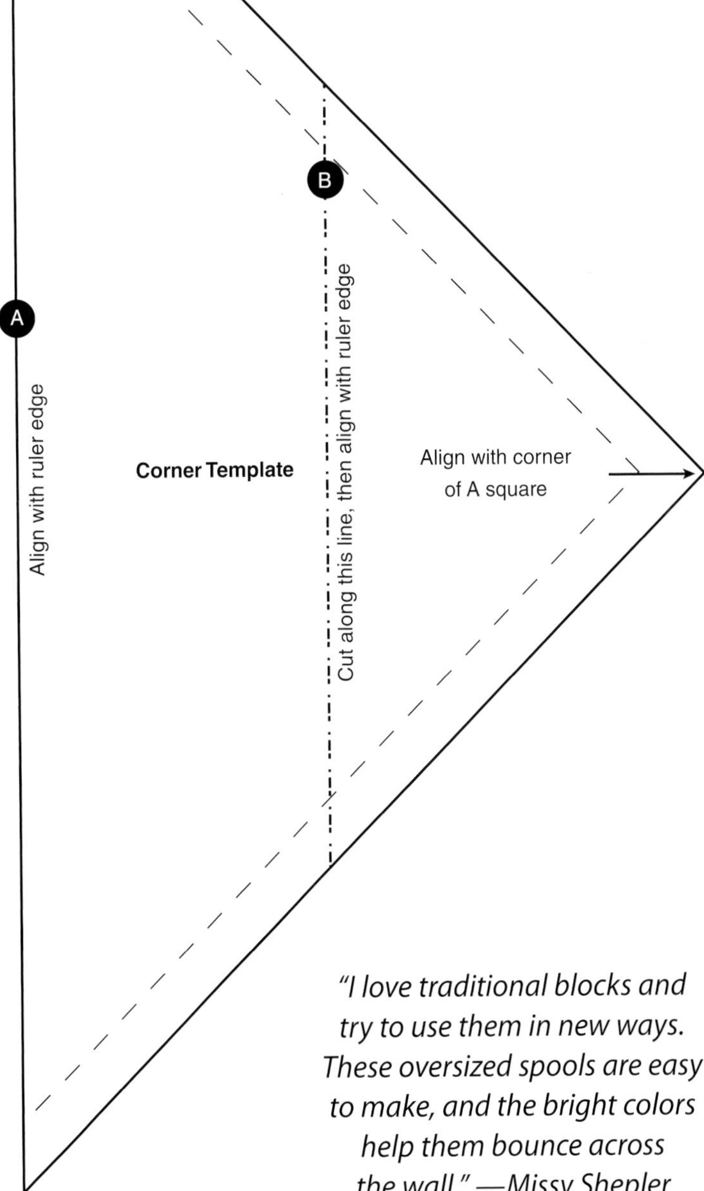

"I love traditional blocks and try to use them in new ways. These oversized spools are easy to make, and the bright colors help them bounce across the wall." —Missy Shepler

Cracked Ice

Design by Connie Kauffman
Machine-Quilted by Vickie Hunsberger

Blue 10" squares and matching yardage were used to make this quilt. Imagine your fabric choice in this pattern.

Project Note

If using precut 10" squares in packages with coordinating purchased border fabrics and fabric for C strips, remove any squares that match the fabric used for the C strips as the pattern will not show if C is the same fabric as any of the A or B triangles.

Project Specifications

- Skill Level: Confident Beginner
- Quilt Size: 83" x 92"
- Block Size: 9" x 9"
- Number of Blocks: 42

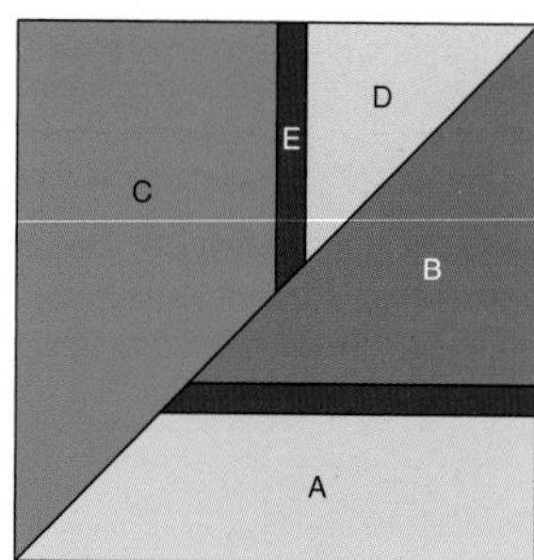

Cracked Ice
9" x 9" Block
Make 42

Materials

- 52 coordinating 10" precut squares
- ½ yard blue tonal 1
- ½ yard blue tonal 2
- 1⅔ yards blue print
- 2 yards dark blue print
- 7¾ yards backing
- Batting 91" x 100"
- Thread
- Large square ruler
- Spray starch and cotton swab or brush (optional)
- Basic sewing tools and supplies

Cutting

1. Select 10 (10") precut squares and cut 40 (2¼" x 10") binding strips.

2. Cut three 3½" by fabric width F1/G1 strips blue tonal 1.

3. Cut three 3½" by fabric width F2/G2 strips blue tonal 2.

4. Cut 14 (1" by fabric width) E strips blue print.

5. Cut seven 5" by fabric width H strips blue print.

6. Cut eight 7½" by fabric width I/J strips dark blue print.

7. Cut three 91" by fabric width strips from backing fabric. Remove selvage edges, join along the 91" lengths and trim to 91" x 100" to make a backing with horizontal seams.

Completing the Blocks

1. Stack four or five squares right side up and cut in half on one diagonal to make two triangles from each fabric; leave in stacks as cut.

2. Measure 3½" from the square corner on one stack of triangles and cut to make A and B pieces as shown in Figure 1; leave pieces as cut.

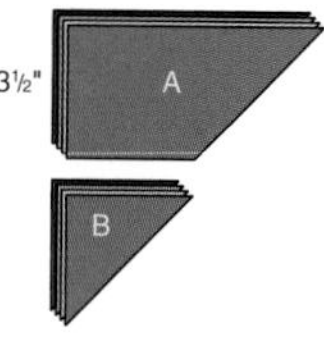

Figure 1

3. Measure down 5½" from the square corner of the second stack of triangles and cut to make C and D pieces referring to Figure 2. Leave pieces as cut.

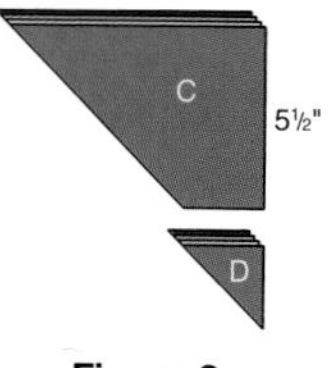

Figure 2

4. Repeat steps 2–4 with remaining squares. Place all A pieces in one stack; repeat with B, C and D pieces.

5. Mix up the pieces within each stack as shown in Figure 3 so that the same fabric pieces will not be sewn together.

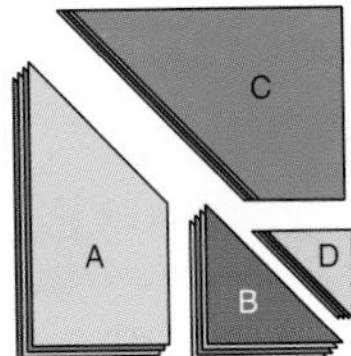

Figure 3

6. Select the top A and B pieces and sew an E strip to the cut edge of the A piece as shown in Figure 4; press seam toward E.

Figure 4

7. Add the B piece to the E side of the unit and press seam toward B as shown in Figure 5.

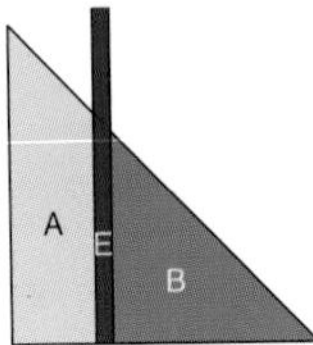

Figure 5

8. Trim the E strip even with the angle of pieces A and B to complete the A-E-B unit as shown in Figure 6.

Make 42

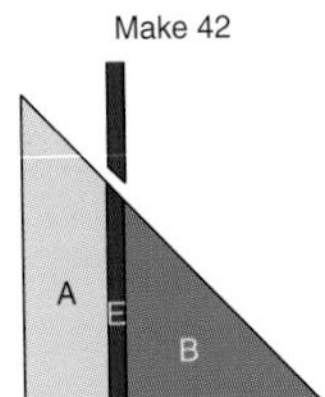

Figure 6

9. Repeat steps 6–8 to make a total of 42 A-E-B units.

10. Repeat steps 6–8 with C and D pieces and E strips to make 42 C-E-D units as shown in Figure 7.

Make 42

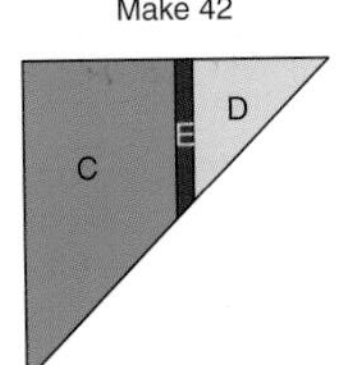

Figure 7

11. Select one each A-E-B and C-E-D unit and join to complete one Cracked Ice block as shown in Figure 8.

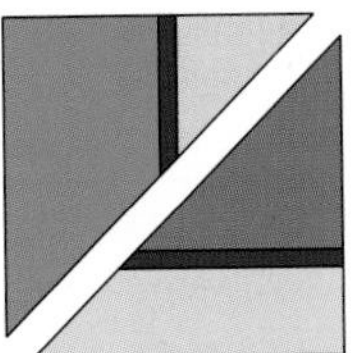
Figure 8

Tip

When sewing bias edges together as in step 11, apply spray starch to the bias edges to help secure these edges during stitching. Spray a little of the starch into the cover cut and use a brush or cotton swab to apply the starch to the bias edges.

12. Square up the block to 9½" x 9½", centering the diagonal seam when trimming as shown in Figure 9.

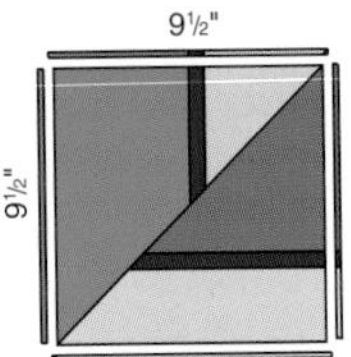

Figure 9

13. Repeat steps 11 and 12 to complete a total of 42 Cracked Ice blocks.

Completing the Quilt

1. Arrange and join the Cracked Ice blocks in seven rows of six blocks each, turning blocks as needed in rows referring to the Assembly Diagram for positioning of blocks; press. ***Note:*** *Try to arrange blocks so the same fabric is not side by side.*

2. Join the rows referring to the Assembly Diagram to complete the pieced center; press.

3. Join the F1/G1 strips on short ends to make a long strip; press. Subcut strips into one 3½" x 63½" F1 strip and one 3½" x 60½" G1 strip.

4. Repeat step 3 with F2/G2 strips.

5. Sew F1 to one side and F2 to the opposite side and G1 and G2 strips to the top and bottom of the pieced center; press seams toward strips.

6. Join the H strips on short ends to make a long strip; press. Subcut strip into four 5" x 69½" H strips.

7. Sew an H strip to opposite sides and then to the top and bottom of the pieced center; press seams toward strips.

8. Join the I/J strips on short ends to make a long strip; press. Subcut strip into two 6½" x 78½" I strips and two 6½" x 83½" J strips.

9. Sew I strips to opposite sides and J strips to the top and bottom of the pieced center to complete the pieced top; press seams toward I and J strips.

10. Layer, quilt and bind referring to Finishing Your Quilt on page 48. ■

"This design was created to use the most from each 10" square. After laying out the blocks it was a surprise to see the zigzag pattern that was in the design. The blue and white fabrics with all the strips and angles brought to mind cracked ice, which became the name." —Connie Kauffman

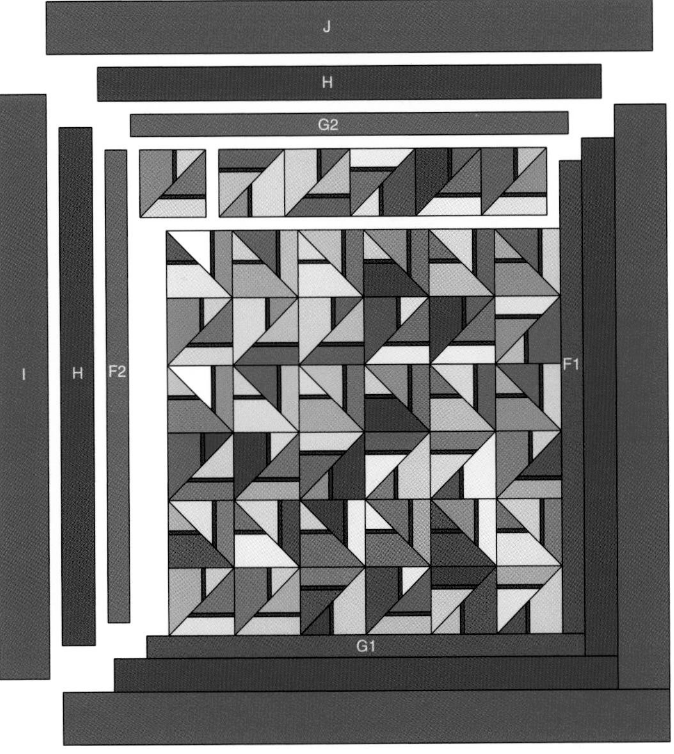

Cracked Ice
Assembly Diagram 83" x 92"

Crumbled Cake

Design by Carolyn S. Vagts for The Village Pattern Company

Try free-form piecing using 10" squares. Discover just how easy it is to create unique blocks. Just trim to size after the block is pieced.

Project Specifications

- Skill Level: Intermediate
- Quilt Size: 58½" x 78½"
- Block Size: 9" x 9"
- Number of Blocks: 35

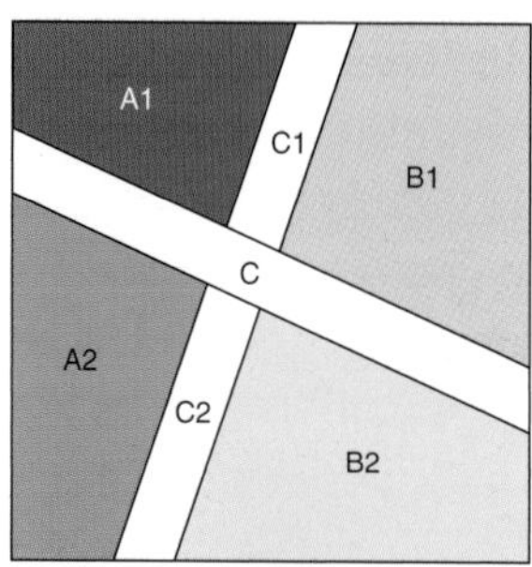

Crumb
9" x 9" Block
Make 35

Materials

- 35 coordinating precut 10" squares
- 1⅔ yards orange tonal
- 2⅓ yards white solid
- 5 yards backing
- Batting 66" x 86"
- Thread
- Basic sewing tools and supplies

Cutting

From orange tonal:

1. Cut seven 4¼" by fabric width G/H strips orange tonal.

2. Cut seven 2¼" by fabric width binding strips orange tonal.

3. Cut three 14" by fabric width strips white solid; subcut into 70 (1½" x 14") C strips.

4. Cut one 9½" by fabric width strip white solid: subcut into 28 (1½" x 9½") D sashing strips.

5. Cut 13 (1½" by fabric width) E/F strips white solid.

6. Cut two 86" strips backing fabric. Remove selvage edges and join along 86" lengths; trim to 66" x 86" to make a backing with vertical seams.

Completing the Blocks

1. Select four 10" squares; stack right side up, aligning edges. Cut apart from top to bottom at an angle as shown in Figure 1 to make A and B sections.

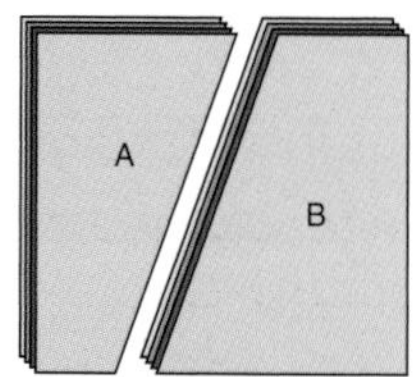

Figure 1

2. Move the top A piece to the bottom of the stack. ***Note:*** *This will make each pair different pieces in the stack as you stitch as shown in Figure 2.*

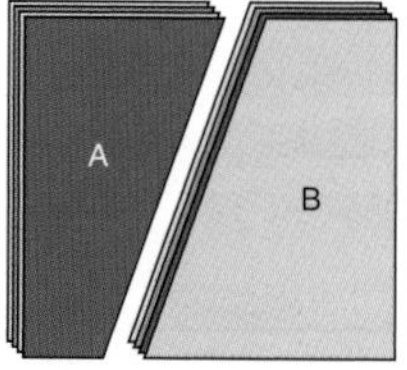

Figure 2

3. Select the top A and B sections (now two different fabrics) from the stacks. Center and sew a C strip to the A section as shown in Figure 3; press seam toward C.

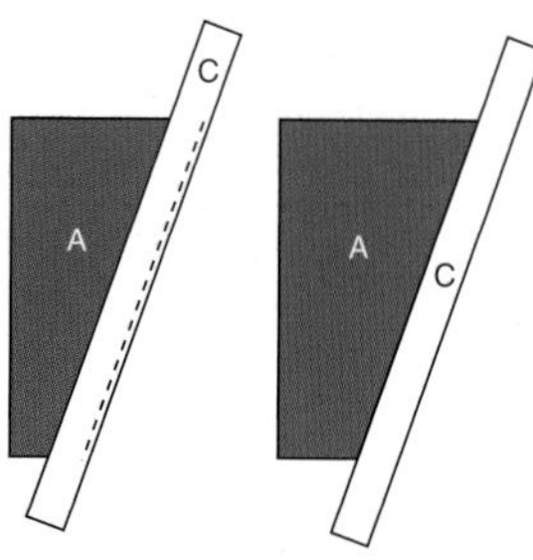

Figure 3

4. Center and sew the B section to the A-C unit and press seam toward C to complete an A-C-B unit as shown in Figure 4.

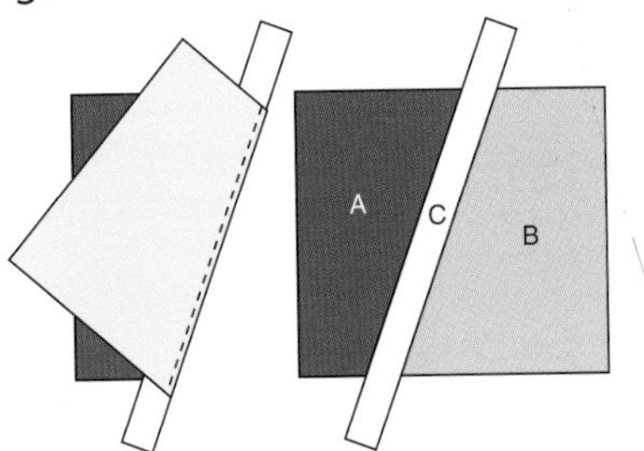

Figure 4

5. Repeat steps 3 and 4 with remaining A and B sections from the stacks.

6. Stack the stitched units, aligning C strips vertically; cut side to side at an angle through the stack as shown in Figure 5 to make an A1-C1-B1 section and an A2-C2-B2 section.

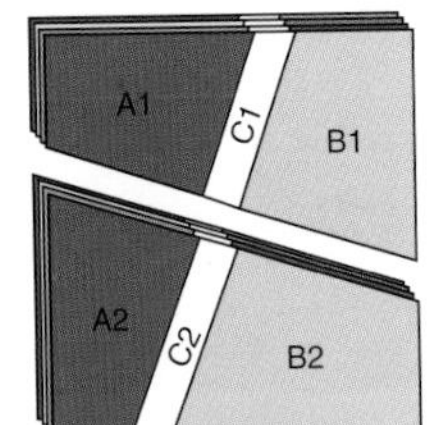

Figure 5

7. Move the top A2-C2-B2 section to the bottom of the stack.

8. Select the top A1-C1-B1 and A2-C2-B2 sections, and center and sew a C strip between the sections, aligning the C1/C2 strips as shown in Figure 6; press seams toward the C strip.

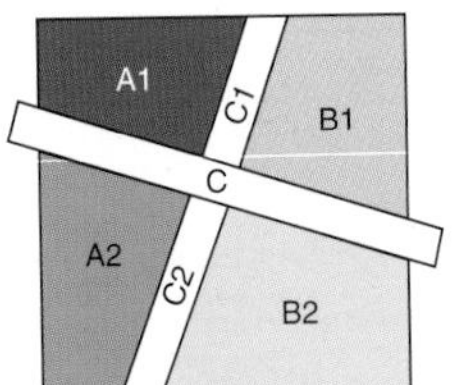

Figure 6

9. Trim the stitched unit to 9½" x 9½" to complete one Crumb block as shown in Figure 7.

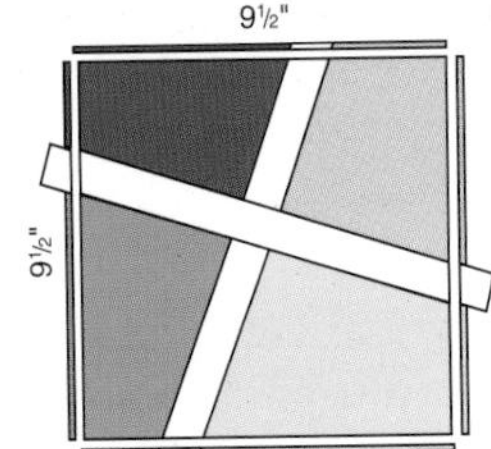

Figure 7

10. Repeat steps 8 and 9 with the remaining stitched sections to complete a total of four Crumb blocks.

11. Repeat steps 1–10 to complete a total of 35 blocks. ***Note:*** *One stack will have three squares instead of four to make 35 blocks.*

Completing the Quilt

1. Select and join five Crumb blocks and four D strips to make a row referring to the Assembly Diagram; press seams toward D. Repeat to make seven rows.

2. Join the E/F strips to make a long strip; press. Subcut strip into eight 1½" x 49½" E strips and two 1½" x 71½" F strips.

3. Join the rows with the E strips, starting and ending with a strip; press seams toward E. Add the F strips to opposite long sides; press seams toward F.

Crumbled Cake
Placement Diagram 58½" x 78½"

4. Join the G/H strips to make a long strip; press. Subcut strip into two 4¼" x 71½" G strips and two 4¼" x 59" H strips.

5. Sew G strips to opposite sides and H strips to the top and bottom of the pieced center to complete the quilt top.

6. Layer, quilt and bind referring to Finishing Your Quilt on page 48. ■

"It's fun to play with 10" squares when trying free-form piecing. There's no need to measure each cut. The beauty is in how each block is similar, yet each block is a bit different." —Carolyn S. Vagts

Tip

When joining the A-C-B units with C, center and sew C to the cut side of one unit. Press and lay the unit on a flat surface and place pins at the edges of the seams between C and the A and B pieces to extend beyond the strip. Place the second unit right sides together on top, aligning the C strip with the pins to perfectly align the C strips from unit to unit referring to Figure 8.

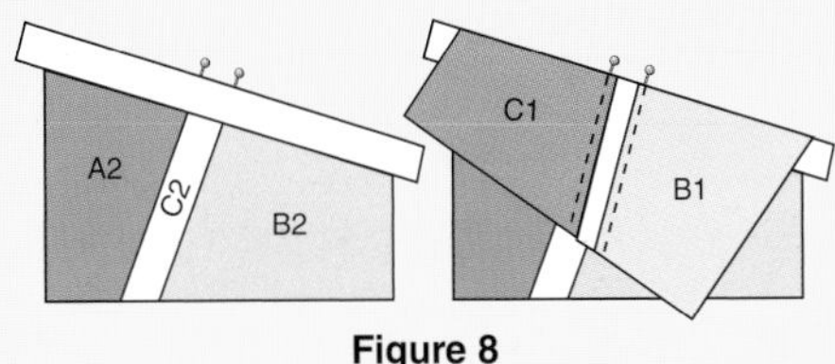

Figure 8

Crumbled Cake Alternate Size
Assembly Diagram 78½" x 98½"
Make 28 more blocks and join in 9 rows of 7 blocks each to create a bed-size quilt using the same-width border strips as the smaller-size quilt. Remember to increase fabric yardages to make this larger-size quilt.

Crumbled Cake Alternate Size
Assembly Diagram 35" x 45"
Make just 12 blocks and join in 4 rows of 3 blocks each and reduce the size of the outer border strip to a 2" finished width to make a baby quilt. You will need less fabric to make this smaller-size quilt.

Progression

Design by Missy Shepler

Precut 10" squares are perfect for this quilt, and cutting is kept to a minimum.

Project Note

This quilt is made up of three different Progression blocks. All blocks start the same way—with a large half-square triangle. Progression 2 and 3 blocks have additional strips. Careful, but not rigid, color placement helps to create a progression of color and value across the quilt. Refer to the Assembly Diagram for color/fabric placement in each block to create the color progression used in the sample quilt.

Project Specifications

- Skill Level: Confident Beginner
- Quilt Size: 59½" x 85"
- Block Size: 8½" x 8½"
- Number of Blocks: 70

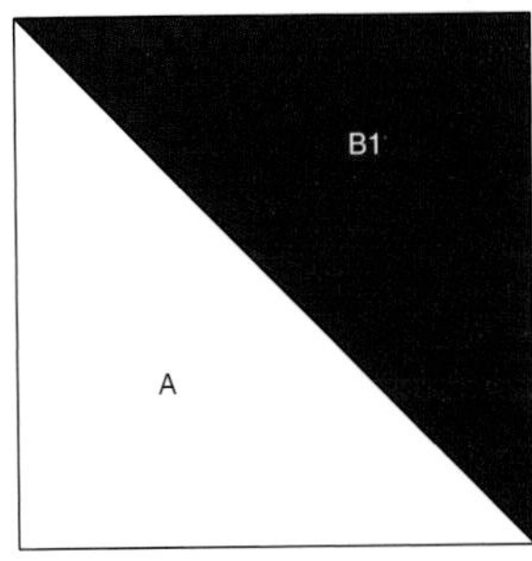

Progression 1
8½" x 8½" Block
Make 30

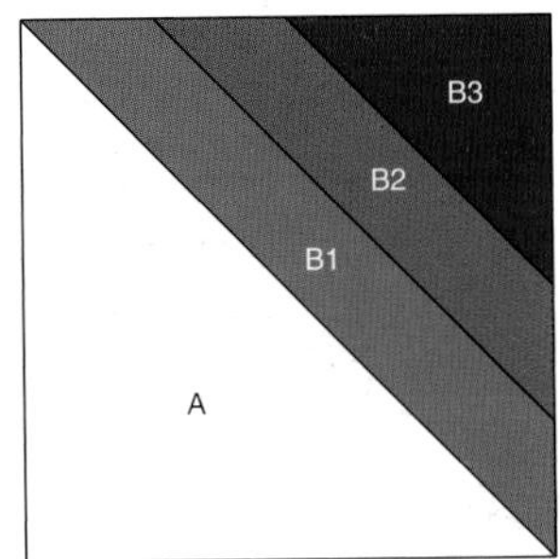

Progression 2
8½" x 8½" Block
Make 20

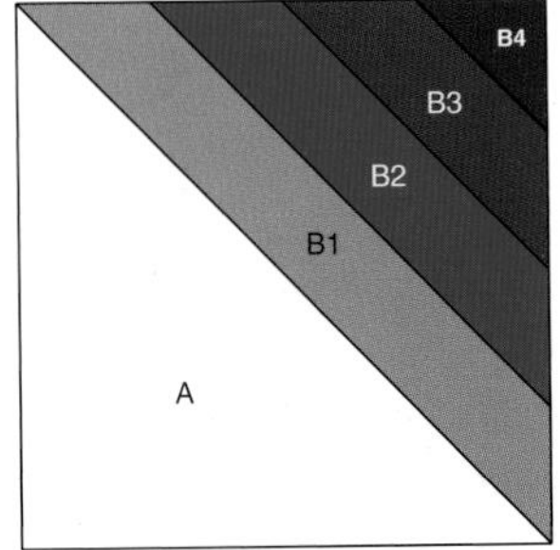

Progression 3
8½" x 8½" Block
Make 20

Materials

- 80 precut 10" batik B squares
- ⅔ yard blue batik
- 2⅞ yards white solid
- 5⅜ yards backing
- Batting 68" x 93"
- Thread
- Basic sewing tools and supplies

Cutting

1. Cut eight 2¼" by fabric width binding strips blue batik.

2. Cut nine 10" by fabric width strips white solid; subcut into 35 (10") A squares.

3. Cut two 93" by fabric width strips from backing fabric. Remove selvage edges, join along the 93" lengths and trim to 68" x 93" to make a backing with vertical seams.

Completing the Blocks

1. Draw a line from corner to corner on the wrong side of each A square.

2. Place a B square right sides together with an A square matching raw edges. Stitch ¼" on each side of the marked line. Cut apart on the marked line to make two A-B1 block units as shown in Figure 1; press seams open. Repeat with all A and B squares to make a total of 70 A-B1 block units.

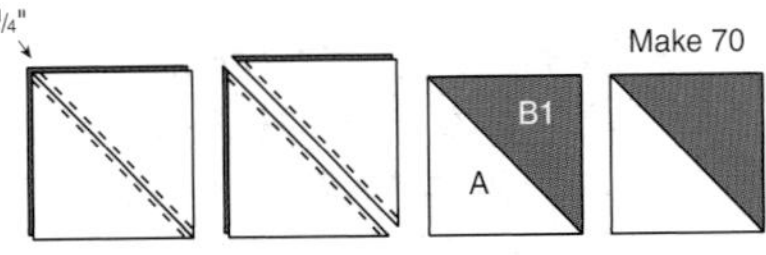

Figure 1

3. Select 30 A-B1 block units for Progression 1 blocks; trim each block to 9" square using the seam between the A and B pieces as a centering guide as shown in Figure 2.

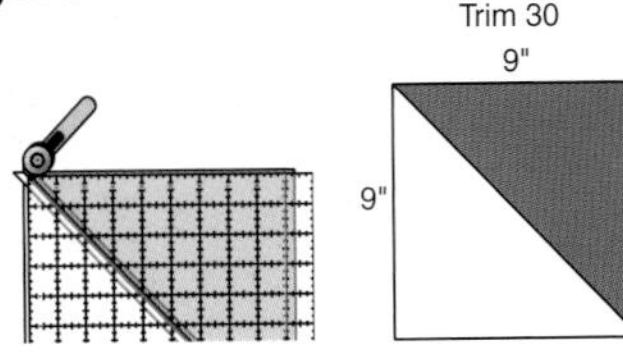

Figure 2

4. From the remaining 40 A-B1 block units, select a unit and draw a line 1½" from the seam line on the wrong side of B1 as shown in Figure 3.

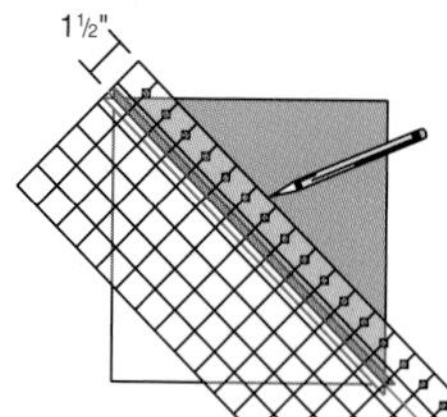

Figure 3

5. Place a B square right sides together with the marked block and with the A-B1 unit on top, stitch on the marked line to create the B2 strip as shown in Figure 4; trim seam allowance to ¼", press B2 to the right side and press seam open. ***Note:*** *To create the color progression in the blocks, pay careful attention to the fabrics used as B2 strips in each block. Refer to color photo of sample quilt for color placement.*

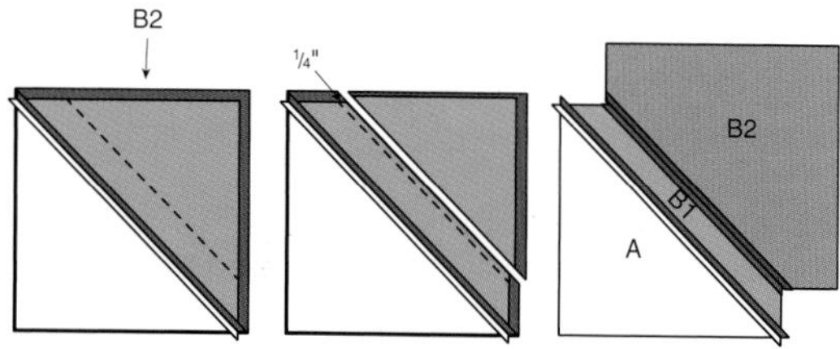

Figure 4

6. Draw a line on the wrong side of the B2 piece 1½" from the B1-B2 seam line as shown in Figure 5; place a B square right sides together with the A-B1-B2 unit and stitch on the marked line to create the B3 strip; trim seam allowance to ¼", press B3 to the right side and press seam open as shown in Figure 6.

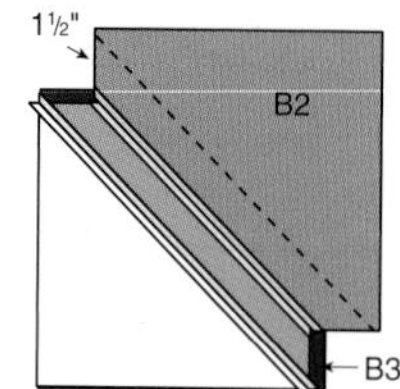

Figure 5

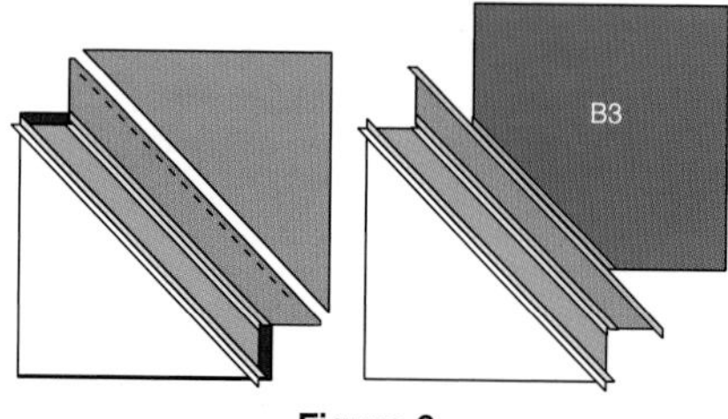

Figure 6

7. Using the diagonal seam between the A and B1 piece as the centering guide, trim the stitched unit to 9" square to complete a Progression 2 block as shown in Figure 7.

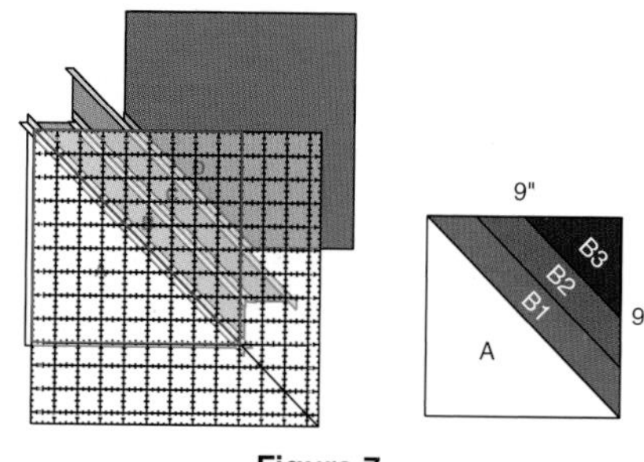

Figure 7

Tip

When using trimmed fabric pieces for strips, make sure that the angled edge of the trimming overlaps the marked line by at least ¼". Check the size of the trimmed fabrics before adding a new strip to a block. With block and strip right sides together, hold fabric together along the seam line. Flip fabrics right side up to ensure that the new strip is large enough to cover the strip area plus the seam allowances.

8. Repeat steps 4–7 to complete a total of 40 A-B1-B2-B3 block units; set aside 20 units for Progression 2 blocks.

9. Select one of the remaining A-B1-B2-B3 block units and mark a line 1½" from the B3 stitching line as in step 4; repeat steps 5 and 7 to add a B4 strip to complete one Progression 3 block referring to Figure 8.

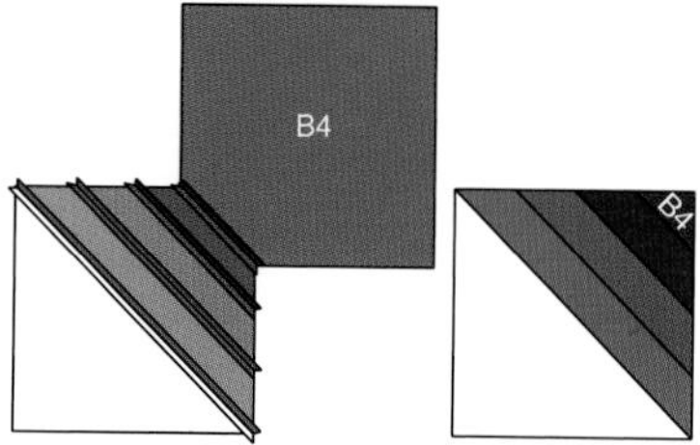

Figure 8

10. Repeat step 9 to complete a total of 20 Progression 3 blocks.

Completing the Quilt

1. Arrange and join 10 Progression 3 blocks to make the vertical row 1 referring to the Assembly Diagram; press seams open.

2. Repeat step 1 with 10 more Progression 3 blocks arranging blocks as shown in the Assembly Diagram to complete the vertical row 2; press seams open.

3. Complete vertical rows 3 and 4 with Progression 2 blocks and vertical rows 5, 6 and 7 with Progression 1 blocks to complete the rows.

4. Arrange and join the rows referring to the Assembly Diagram to complete the quilt top; press.

5. Layer, quilt and bind referring to Finishing Your Quilt on page 48. ■

"I love the graphic look of simple shapes, especially zigzags. The progression of blocks from a simple to a more complex/refined shape adds extra motion and interest." —Missy Shepler

Tip

Working with bias edges can be a bit daunting. By sewing larger pieces in place, and then trimming after the seam is sewn, those bias worries can be placed on the back burner! Blocks are sewn slightly oversized, then trimmed, making it easy to line up seam intersections.

Tip

Precuts are perfect for this project. There's no need to worry about coordinating colors, prints or patterns, and cutting is kept to a minimum. Don't worry if the precuts are not perfectly square. Final blocks are trimmed to a perfect 9" square before quilt top assembly.

Progression
Assembly Diagram 59½" x 85"

Me & My Shadow

Designed & Pieced by Gina Gempesaw
Machine-Quilted by Carole Whaling

Feature your favorite 10" squares in this fabulous quilt. It's quick and easy to piece and can be dramatic if your color choices are bold.

Project Specifications

- Skill Level: Confident Beginner
- Quilt Size: 78½" x 78½"
- Block Size: 14" x 14"
- Number of Blocks: 16

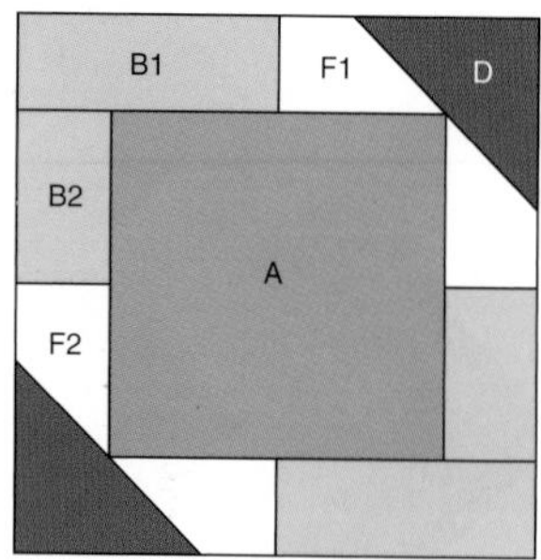

Shadow
14" x 14" Block
Make 16

Materials

- 40–42 assorted 10" batik squares
- ⅔ yard multicolored batik
- 1 yard black solid
- 3⅔ yards white tonal
- 7⅓ yards backing
- Batting 86" x 86"
- Thread
- Basic sewing tools and supplies

Cutting

1. Trim 16 (10") squares to 9½" A squares.

2. From each of 16 (10") squares, cut two each 3" x 7½" B1 rectangles and two 3" x 5" B2 rectangles.

3. Cut 56 (3") C squares from the remaining 10" squares.

4. Cut eight 2¼" by fabric width binding strips multicolored batik.

5. Cut five 5½" by fabric width strips black solid; subcut into 32 (5½") D squares.

6. Cut one 3" by fabric width strip black solid; subcut into nine 3" E squares.

7. Cut two 14½" by fabric width strips white tonal; subcut into 24 (3" x 14½") G strips.

8. Cut three 7½" by fabric width strips white tonal; subcut into 32 (3" x 7½") F1 rectangles. Trim remainder of last strip to 5" and cut four 3" x 5" F2 rectangles.

9. Cut two 5" by fabric width strips white tonal; subcut into 28 additional 3" x 5" F2 rectangles to total 32.

10. Cut seven 2½" by fabric width H/I strips white tonal.

11. Cut four 3" by fabric width strips white tonal; subcut into 56 (3") J squares.

12. Cut eight 3½" by fabric width K/L strips white tonal.

13. Cut three 86" by fabric width strips backing fabric. Remove selvage edges, join along the 86" lengths and trim to 86" x 86" to make a backing with vertical or horizontal seams.

Completing the Blocks

1. Draw a diagonal line from corner to corner on the wrong side of each D square.

2. To complete one Shadow block, select one A square, two each matching B1 and B2 rectangles, two F1 and F2 rectangles and two D squares.

3. Sew B1 to F1 as shown in Figure 1; press. Repeat to make a second B1-F1 unit.

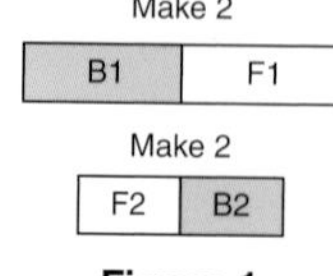

Figure 1

4. Sew B2 to F2, again referring to Figure 1; press. Repeat to make a second B2-F2 unit.

5. Sew a B2-F2 unit to opposite sides of A referring to Figure 2; press seams away from A. Sew the B1-F1 units to the remaining sides of A, again referring to Figure 2; press seams away from A.

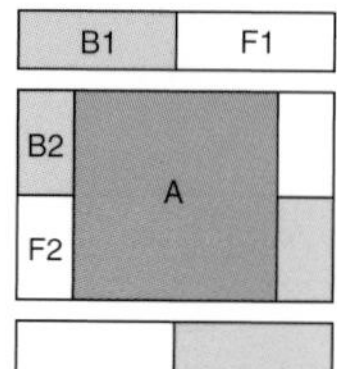

Figure 2

6. Referring to Figure 3, place a D square right sides together on each F corner of the pieced unit and stitch on the marked lines; trim seam allowance to ¼" and press D to the right side to complete one Shadow block.

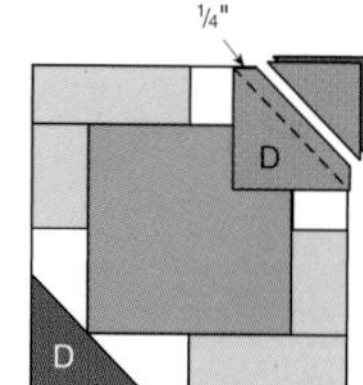

Figure 3

7. Repeat steps 2–6 to complete a total of 16 Shadow blocks.

Completing the Quilt

1. Arrange and join four Shadow blocks with three G strips to make a block row; press seams toward G strips. Repeat to make a total of four block rows.

2. Join three E squares with four G strips to make a sashing row; press seams toward G strips. Repeat to make a total of three sashing rows.

3. Arrange and join the block rows with the sashing rows to complete the pieced center referring to the Assembly Diagram; press seams toward sashing rows.

4. Join the H/I strips on short ends to make a long strip; press. Subcut strips into two 2½" x 64" H strips and two 2½" x 68" I strips.

5. Sew the H strips to opposite sides and I strips to the top and bottom of the pieced center; press seams toward strips.

6. Select and join 13 C squares and 14 J squares, beginning and ending with J, to make a pieced side strip referring to the Assembly Diagram; press seams toward C squares. Repeat to make a second side strip.

7. Sew the pieced strips to opposite sides of the pieced center; press seams toward the H strips.

8. Repeat step 6 with 14 J squares and 15 C squares to make the top strip; press seams toward C. Repeat to make the bottom strip. Sew the pieced strips to the top and bottom of the pieced center; press seams toward I strips.

9. Join the K/L strips to make a long strip; press. Subcut strip into two 3½" x 73" K strips and two 3½" x 79" L strips.

10. Sew the K strips to opposite sides and L strips to the top and bottom of the pieced center to complete the quilt top; press seams toward K and L strips.

11. Layer, quilt and bind referring to Finishing Your Quilt on page 48. ■

Me & My Shadow
Assembly Diagram 78½" x 78½"

Tip

Pair up two contrasting squares from the group of 10" squares for each block. Decide which square becomes the block center and which one becomes the frame.

"A fabric line, as shown in a Layer Cake, usually includes a mix of large- and small-scale prints. This project is intended to feature the large-scale prints while still using the rest of the prints in the quilt." —Gina Gempesaw

Delectable Mountain Getaway

Design by Nancy McNally

Here's a quilt with a bit of a challenge. Just keep in mind the sky and mountains when piecing and arranging placement.

Project Notes

If your 10" precut square packages do not include enough light and dark squares, you may need to purchase extra black and cream batiks to complete the quilt.

Please note that block seams do not align from block to block and that the sashing triangle seams do not match to the block triangle seams.

Project Specifications

- Skill Level: Intermediate/Advanced
- Quilt Size: 99½" x 99½"
- Block Size: 13½" x 8½"
- Number of Blocks: 40

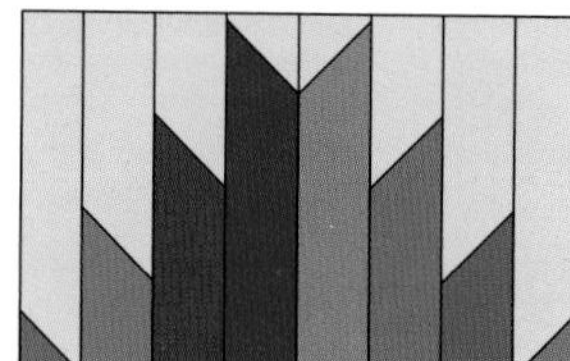

Delectable Mountain
13½" x 8½" Block
Make 40

Materials

- 40 each light and dark 10" precut squares
- 1 yard rust batik
- 2⅛ yards black batik
- 3½ yards cream batik
- 9⅛ yards backing
- Batting 107" x 107"
- Thread
- Cutting mat and rotary cutter
- Basic sewing tools and supplies

Cutting

1. Cut 10 (2¼" by fabric width) binding strips rust batik.

2. Cut two 9⅜" by fabric width strips black batik; subcut into eight 9⅜" B squares.

3. Cut one 7⅝" by fabric width strip black batik; subcut into two 7⅝" K squares and two 3⅞" F squares.

4. Cut three 2¼" by fabric width strips black batik; subcut into 48 (2¼") D squares.

5. Cut eight 3½" by fabric width E strips black batik.

6. Cut two 9⅜" by fabric width strips cream batik; subcut into eight 9⅜" A squares.

7. Cut one 7⅝" by fabric width strip cream batik; subcut into two 7⅝" J squares and two 3⅞" G squares.

8. Cut six 4" by fabric width strips cream batik; subcut into 24 (4" x 9") C rectangles.

9. Cut 10 (6½" by fabric width) H/I strips cream batik.

10. Cut three 107" by fabric width strips backing fabric. Remove selvage, join along the 107" lengths and trim to 107" x 107" to make a backing with vertical or horizontal seams.

Completing the Delectable Mountain Blocks

1. Trim each 10" precut square to 9⅜" square.

2. Separate the precut squares into 40 each light and dark squares.

3. Draw a diagonal line from corner to corner on the wrong side of each light square.

4. Place a light square right sides together with a dark square and stitch ¼" on each side of the marked line. Referring to Figure 1, cut apart on the marked line to make two light/dark half-square triangle units; press seams toward dark triangles. Repeat to make a total of 80 units.

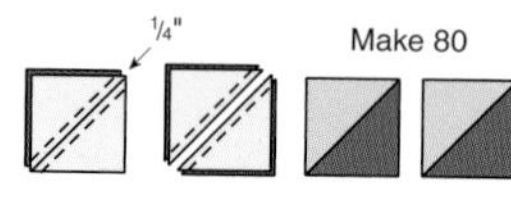

Figure 1

5. Lay out the half-square triangle units in two stacks of 40 units each with darks facing right in one pile and lights facing left in the second pile referring to Figure 2. ***Note:*** *Your stacks will look like a mountain.*

Figure 2

6. Select one each right-facing and left-facing unit. Place right side up in the same position on the cutting mat as shown in Figure 2 and subcut each unit into four 2¼" segments each as shown in Figure 3.

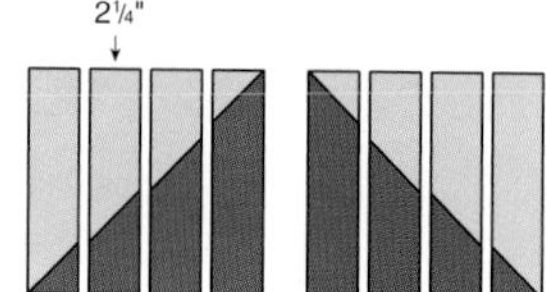

Figure 3

7. Repeat step 6 with all units.

8. Stack four or five cut units to make several piles as shown in Figure 4.

Figure 4

9. Carefully pick up the last stack on the far left and swap places with the stack on the far right as shown in Figure 5.

Figure 5

10. Repeat swapping the pieces in subsequent stacks so your pieces are arranged as shown in Figure 6.

Figure 6

11. Repeat steps 8–10 until all units are in stacks and pieces have been swapped to look like Figure 6.

12. To achieve a scrappy look, swap the pieces around in each stack to bring colors from the bottom to the top referring to Figure 7.

Figure 7

13. Select one piece from each stack for one block. Join adjacent pieces in sets of two, and then join those units to make two block halves referring to Figure 8; join the halves to complete one block referring to Figure 9. Press seams open.

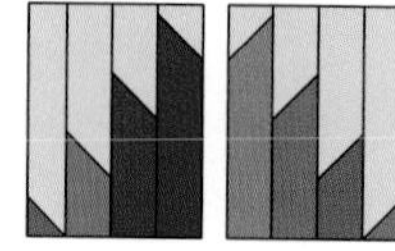
Figure 8

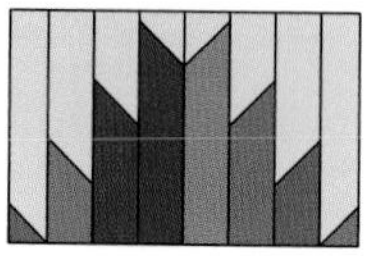

Figure 9

14. Repeat step 13 to complete a total of 40 Delectable Mountain blocks.

15. Trim blocks to 14" x 9".

Completing the Triangle Units

1. Repeat steps 3 and 4 of Completing the Delectable Mountain Blocks using the A and B squares to complete a total of 16 A-B triangle units referring to Figure 10.

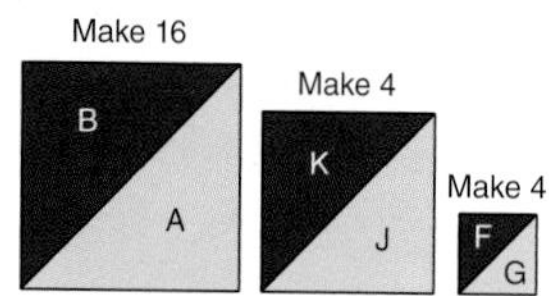

Figure 10

2. Repeat step 1 using J and K squares to make four J-K triangle units, and with F and G squares to make four F-G units, again referring to Figure 10.

Completing the Sashing Units

1. Draw a diagonal line from corner to corner on the wrong side of each D square.

2. Place a D square right sides together on one end of a C rectangle and stitch on the marked line; trim seam allowance to ¼" as shown in Figure 11 and press D to the right side.

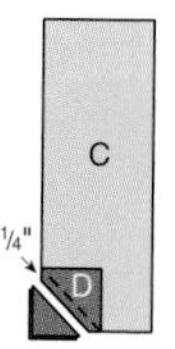

Figure 11

3. Repeat step 2 with a second D square on the adjacent corner of C to complete a C-D sashing unit as shown in Figure 12.

4. Repeat steps 2 and 3 to complete a total of 24 C-D sashing units.

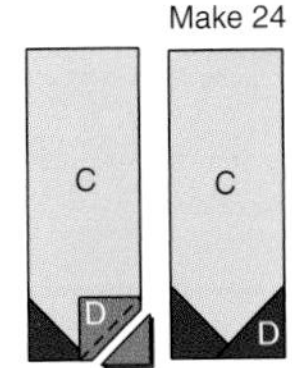

Figure 12

Completing the Quilt

1. Arrange and join the four J-K triangle units to complete the quilt center unit referring to the Assembly Diagram for positioning; press.

2. Arrange and join the A-B triangle units with the Delectable Mountain blocks and the C-D sashing units to make rows referring to the Assembly Diagram for positioning of blocks and units; press. ***Note:*** *The top of the small triangles at each end of the blocks will not match to the top of the corner triangles on the C-D sashing units as shown in Figure 13. Block seams will not match from row to row.*

Figure 13

3. Stitch a block to opposite sides and then a row to the top and bottom of the quilt center unit referring to the Assembly Diagram. Stitch remaining rows to sides and then top and bottom of pieced center unit, again referring to the Assembly Diagram, to complete the pieced center; press.

4. Join the E strips on short ends to make a long strip; press. Subcut strips into four 3½" x 82" E strips.

5. Sew an E strip to opposite sides of the pieced center; press seams toward E.

6. Sew an F-G triangle unit to each end of each remaining E strip referring to the Assembly Diagram for positioning of units; press seams toward E. Sew these strips to the top and bottom of the pieced center; press seams toward E.

7. Join the H/I strips on short ends to make a long strip; press. Subcut strip into two 6½" x 88" H strips and two 6½" x 100" I strips.

8. Sew H strips to the top and bottom and I strips to opposite sides of the pieced center to complete the pieced top; press seams toward H and I strips.

9. Layer, quilt and bind referring to Finishing Your Quilt on page 48. ■

Tip

Precut fabric packages of any size include an unknown number of light, medium and dark pieces. If a pattern of lights and darks is important, you might need to precut your own same-size pieces to add to the purchased packages to complete your quilt. This quilt requires the same number of light and dark squares. If your precut packages do not have the required number, cut the extras needed from yardage.

Delectable Mountain Getaway
Assembly Diagram 99½" x 99½"

"My inspiration for this quilt came from the warm, inviting and rich colors of fall, and the contrast between mountains and the sky. By using lights and darks from precut collections, a step was already done. Have fun!" —Nancy McNally

Woven Paths

Designed and Quilted by Sandra L. Hatch

It's easy to cut up 10" squares to create a really scrappy-looking quilt even without a stash of scraps!

Project Specifications

- Skill Level: Confident Beginner
- Quilt Size: 74" x 84"
- Block Size: 9½" x 9½"
- Number of Blocks: 30

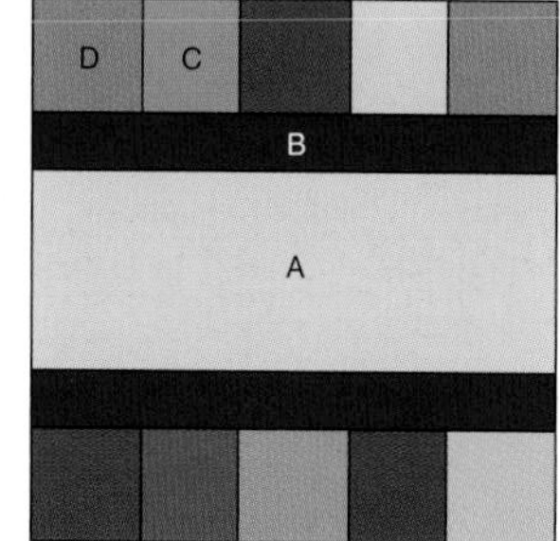

Woven Paths
9½" x 9½" Block
Make 30

Materials

- 42 assorted coordinating 10" squares
- 2⅛ yards navy batik
- 2⅓ yards navy paisley
- 5¼ yards backing fabric
- Batting 82" x 92"
- Thread to match fabrics
- Basic sewing tools and supplies

Cutting

From 10" squares:

1. Cut one 4" x 10" A rectangle from each of 30 (10") squares.

2. Cut the remainder of each of the squares into one 2½" x 10" strip and one 2¼" x 10" strip. Subcut each 2½" x 10" strip into four 2½" D squares (120 total). Subcut each 2¼" x 10" strip into four 2¼" x 2½" C rectangles (120 total).

3. Cut each of the remaining 12 (10") squares into four 2½" x 10" strips. Subcut strips into a total of 192 (2½") D squares. ***Note:*** *You need 294 total D squares; you will have extra squares to move around as needed for variety.*

4. Cut three 10" by fabric width strips navy batik; subcut into 60 (1½" x 10") B strips.

5. Cut three 1¾" by fabric width E strips navy batik.

6. Cut three 2" by fabric width F strips navy batik.

7. Cut eight 2¼" by fabric width binding strips navy batik.

8. Cut two 10½" x 64½" G strips and two 10½" x 74½" H strips along the length of the navy paisley.

9. Cut two 92" by fabric width strips from backing fabric. Remove selvage edges, join along the 92" lengths and trim to 82" x 92" to make a backing with vertical seams.

Completing the Blocks

1. Select one A rectangle, two B strips, four C rectangles and six D squares to complete one Woven Paths block.

2. To complete one block, sew a B strip to opposite sides of A referring to Figure 1; press seams toward B.

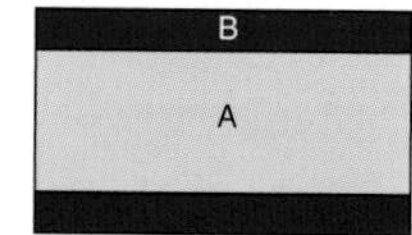

Figure 1

3. Join two C rectangles and three D squares to make a C-D strip as shown in Figure 2; press seams in one direction. Repeat to make a second C-D strip.

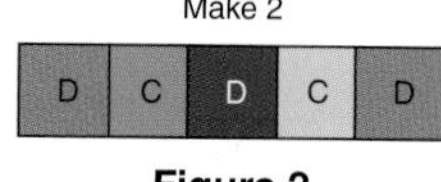

Figure 2

4. Sew a C-D strip to opposite sides of the A-B unit to complete one Woven Paths block referring to Figure 3; press seams toward B.

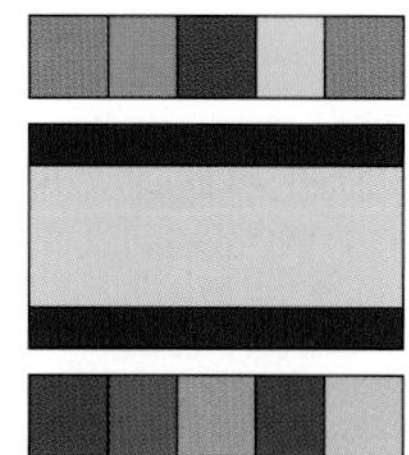

Figure 3

5. Repeat steps 1–4 to complete a total of 30 Woven Paths blocks.

Completing the Quilt

1. Arrange and join five Woven Paths blocks to make a block row, turning the blocks referring to the Assembly Diagram. Repeat to make a total of six block rows. Press seams in adjacent rows in opposite directions.

2. Join the rows to complete the pieced center; press seams in one direction.

3. Join the E strips on short ends to make a long strip; press. Subcut strip into two 1¾" x 57½" E strips.

4. Sew an E strip to opposite long sides of the pieced center; press seams toward strips.

5. Join the F strips on short ends to make a long strip; press. Subcut strip into two 2" x 50½" F strips.

6. Sew an F strip to the top and bottom of the pieced center; press seams toward strips.

7. Select and join 30 D squares to make a pieced side strip; press seams in one direction. Repeat to make a second side strip.

8. Sew a pieced side strip to opposite sides of the pieced center; press seams toward E strips.

9. Select and join 27 D squares to make the pieced top strip; press seams in one direction. Repeat to make the bottom strip. Sew these strips to the top and bottom of the pieced center; press seams toward F strips.

10. Sew a G strip to opposite sides and the H strips to the top and bottom of the pieced center to complete the quilt top; press seams toward strips.

11. Layer, quilt and bind referring to Finishing Your Quilt on page 48. ■

"I love combining print fabrics with batiks. In this quilt, I expanded the variety of fabrics in the print collection to include coordinating batiks. It was fun to treat these 10" squares as scraps and to select them randomly to make the blocks and border strips." —Sandra L. Hatch

Tip

Separate the C rectangles and D squares into separate bags and shake them up. When one of these pieces is needed, reach your hand into the bag and pull out a piece. If you have two of the same fabric next to each other, put it back into the bag and choose another. This takes all the stress out of making decisions about the placement of the squares and rectangles.

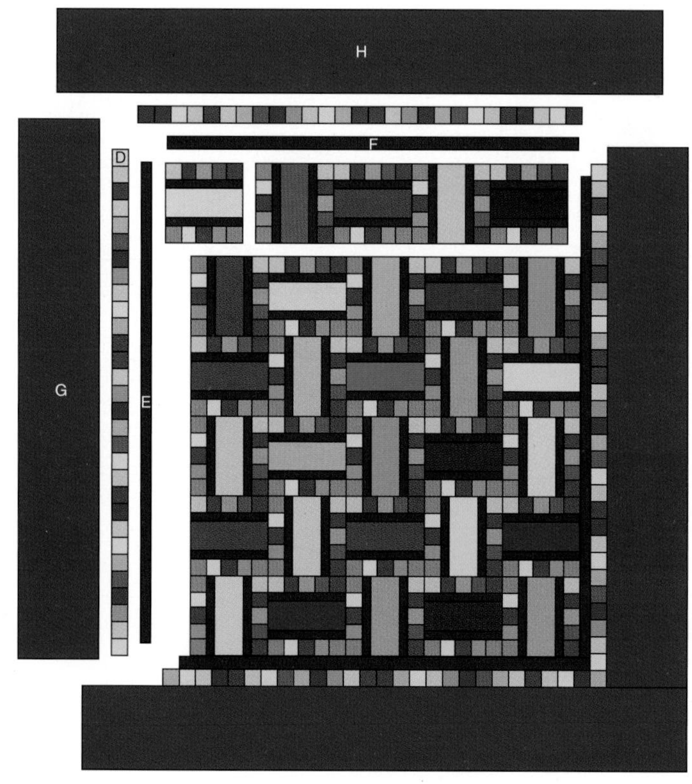

Woven Paths
Assembly Diagram 74" x 84"

Precut 10" Squares Chart

You may cut 10" squares into many different configurations. The illustrations below show a few of the choices. What is not shown is how these can be used to cut a variety of appliqué shapes or other pieced template shapes used to make quilts.

Using the precut 10" squares allows you the variety of using an assortment of coordinated fabrics in your quilts without purchasing lots of yardage. Whether you use them to make the quilts in this book or in other projects, adding precut squares to your fabric collection will broaden the assortment of colors and prints in your stash.

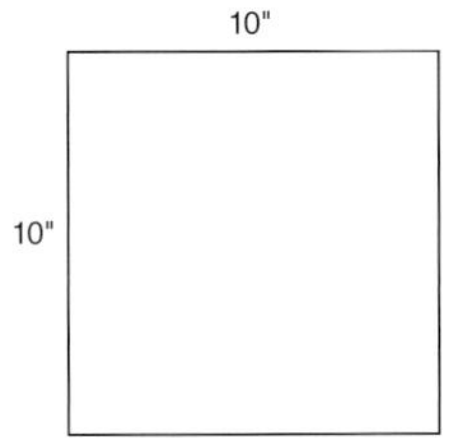

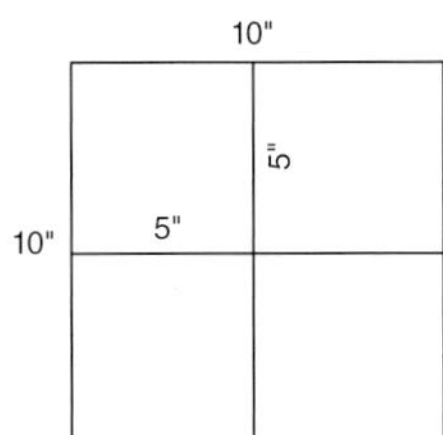

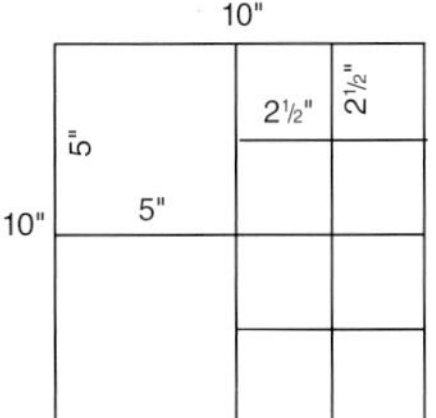

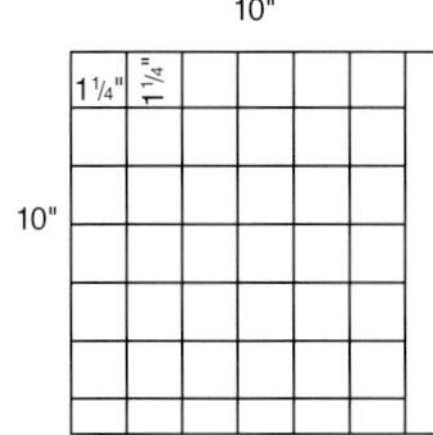

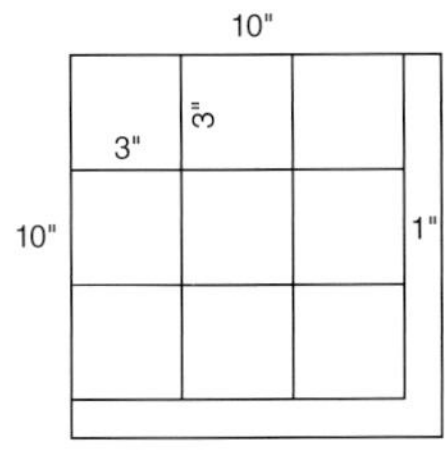

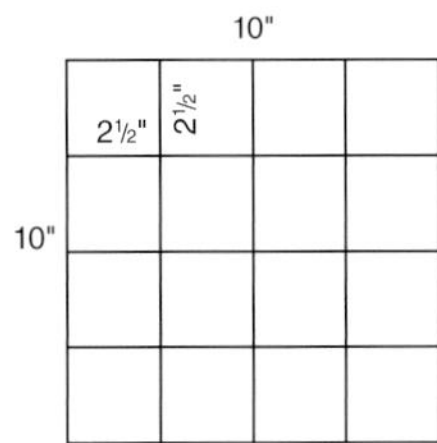

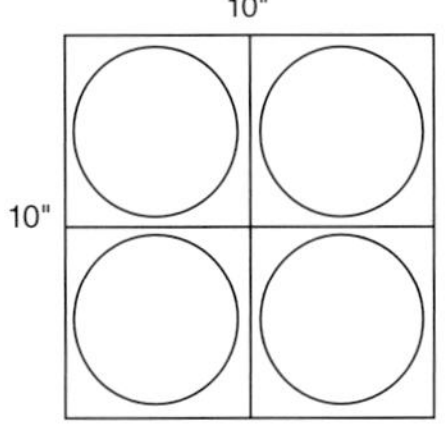

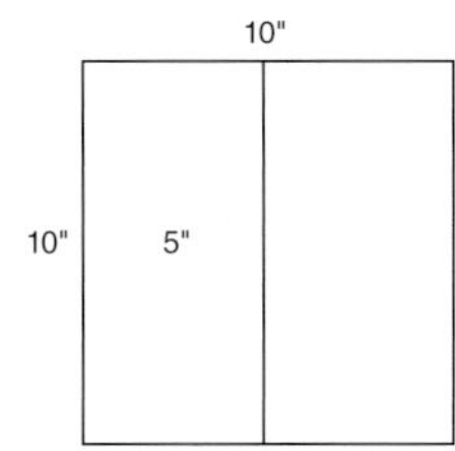

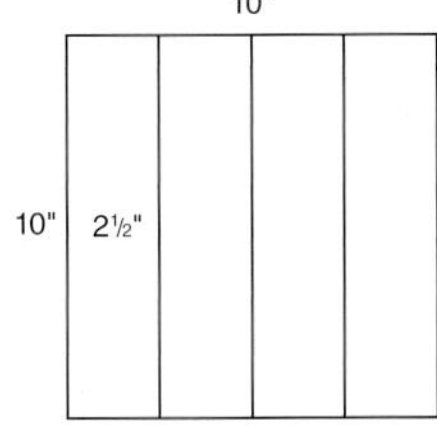

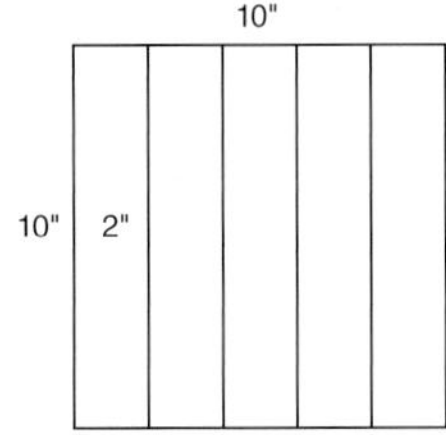

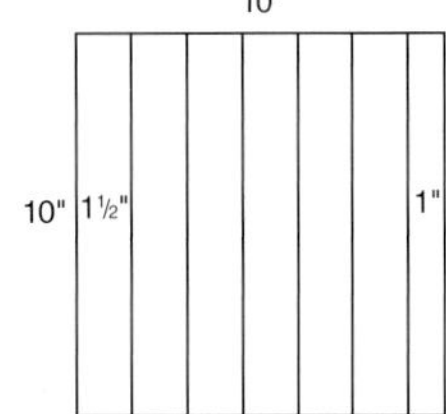

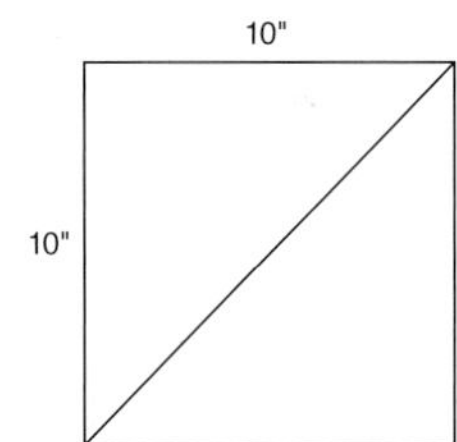

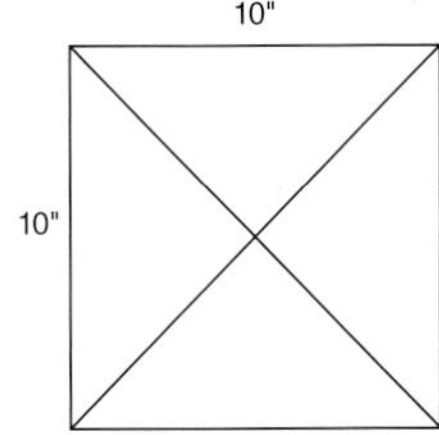

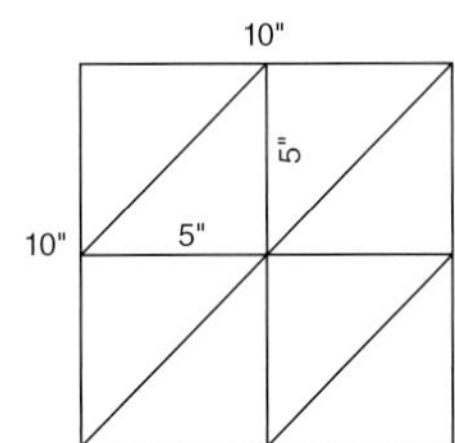

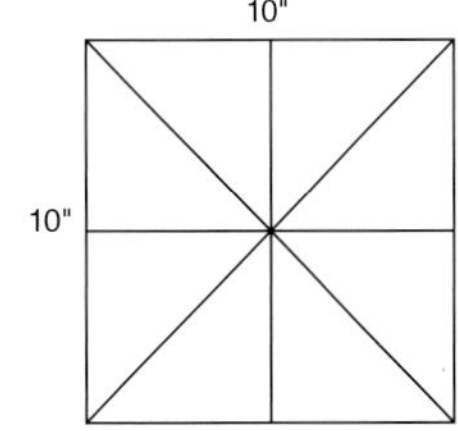

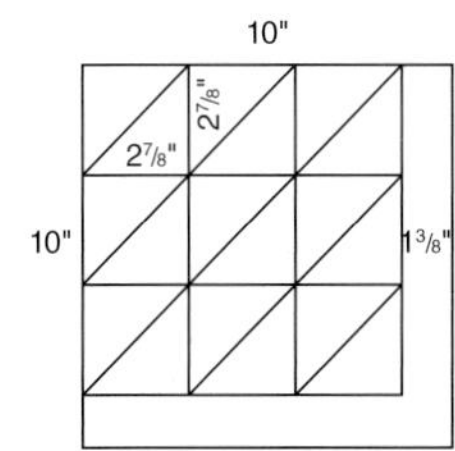

Special Thanks

Please join us in thanking the talented quilt designers whose work is featured in this collection.

Gina Gempesaw
Me & My Shadow, page 36
Quick Chic, page 3

Sandra L. Hatch
Woven Paths, page 44

Connie Kauffman
Cracked Ice, page 24

Chris Malone
Pop of Color Bed Runner & Pillow, page 10

Nancy McNally
Delectable Mountain Getaway, page 40

Missy Shepler
Progression, page 33
Sparkling Spools, page 20

Wendy Sheppard
Sunburst Melody, page 15

Carolyn S. Vagts
Crumbled Cake, page 28

Julie Weaver
Beanstalks, page 6

Fabric & Supplies

We would like to thank the following manufacturers who provided materials for our designers to make sample projects for this book.

Beanstalks, page 6: Simply Color and Bella Solids fabric collections from Moda; Thermore® batting from Hobbs.

Cracked Ice, page 24: Spa fabric collection by Deb Strain from Moda; Cotton and PolyLite threads from Sulky®; Soft & Bright batting from The Warm Company.

Crumbled Cake, page 28: Flirt fabric collection from Moda; Quilter's Dream Wool batting.

Delectable Mountain Getaway, page 40: Bali Tiramisu Crackers (10" squares) from Hoffman.

Pop of Color Bed Runner & Pillow, page 10: Chateau Rouge fabric collection from Moda.

Progression, page 33: Coastal Tonga Treat Squares and Soho Cotton Solids from Timeless Treasures.

Sparkling Spools, page 20: Bazaar Tonga Treat Squares and Soho Cotton Solids from Timeless Treasures.

Sunburst Melody, page 15: Hello Sunshine and Good Life fabric collections from Riley Blake Designs; Tuscany Silk batting from Hobbs; Aurifil Mako 50 cotton thread.

Woven Paths, page 44: Coventry Court fabric collection and coordinating Artisan Batiks from Robert Kaufman; Soft Touch® cotton batting from Fairfield; Star Machine Quilting thread from Coats, distributed by YLI.

Finishing Your Quilt

1. Press quilt top on both sides; check for proper seam pressing and trim all loose threads.

2. Sandwich batting between the stitched top and the prepared backing piece; pin or baste layers together to hold. Mark quilting design and quilt as desired by hand or machine.

3. When quilting is complete, remove pins or basting. Trim batting and backing fabric edges even with raw edges of quilt top.

4. Join binding strips on short ends with diagonal seams to make one long strip; trim seams to ¼" and press seams open.

5. Fold the binding strip in half with wrong sides together along length; press.

6. Sew binding to quilt edges, matching raw edges, mitering corners and overlapping ends.

7. Fold binding to the back side and stitch in place to finish.

Annie's®

Sweet Layer Cakes is published by Annie's, 306 East Parr Road, Berne, IN 46711. Printed in USA.

ISBN: 978-1-59635-646-7
2 3 4 5 6 7 8 9